# LUBETKIN AND GOLDFINGER

# LUBETKIN AND GOLDFINGER

## THE RISE AND FALL OF BRITISH HIGH-RISE COUNCIL HOUSING

Nicholas Russell

The Book Guild Ltd

First published in Great Britain in 2023 by
The Book Guild Ltd
Unit E2 Airfield Business Park,
Harrison Road, Market Harborough,
Leicestershire. LE16 7UL
Tel: 0116 2792299
www.bookguild.co.uk
Email: info@bookguild.co.uk
Twitter: @bookguild

Typeset in 11pt Minion Pro

Printed and bound by CPI Group (UK) Ltd, Croydon, CR0 4YY

ISBN 978 1915603 746

British Library Cataloguing in Publication Data.
A catalogue record for this book is available from the British Library.

*Dedicated to my volunteer colleagues,*
*who bring historic sites to life*

# CONTENTS

High-rise towers and slab blocks of council flats, relics from the mid-twentieth century, are dotted all over the country. For many people they are symbols of deprivation, overrun with antisocial children and drug-dealing teenagers who terrorise the local population. They ask how such abominations could have been built. The culprits must be arrogant architects and town planners of the modernist architectural school in league with unfeeling local politicians who filled the towers with poverty-stricken, dysfunctional families. What were they all thinking?

And yet high-rise residential towers are going up again in city centres, not for working-class council tenants but ambitious young professionals who want to live close to the facilities only cities can provide. High-rise was and still is an important part of any solution to housing people decently in big towns and cities.

The designers of mid-twentieth century high-rise council homes were not really to blame for their demise. It was the result of cost-cutting and neglect by local authorities struggling to cope with the costs of the social breakdown from unemployment and homelessness in the late 1970s and '80s. The situation was not helped by the slow loss of faith in any role for the state in housing after its high point during the Labour administration of 1945–51.

Many of the architects concerned have been relegated to the sidelines. This is true of Berthold Lubetkin and Ernö Goldfinger, idealistic communists who migrated from central Europe, arriving here in the 1930s. They might have had important roles in the design of post-war council housing. They thoroughly understood the virtues of a key construction material at the time, steel-reinforced concrete, which allowed tall towers to be built for a reasonable price. They also realised that residents should feel emotionally engaged with their homes and tried to ensure the ones they built were welcoming places.

In practice they took only minor roles in the post-war high-rise boom because their design principles, aesthetic concerns and belief in quality reduced their opportunities as pressure increased to build homes cheaply and fast. Lubetkin is well known for the aphorism that 'nothing is too good for ordinary people', but the cost of providing quality accommodation for everyone proved beyond this country's political will and economic capacity then (and now).

This book tells the story of Lubetkin and Goldfinger with the aim of restoring their reputations. They were almost the same age, shared elements of architectural training and worked with similar design principles. They both came from wealthy assimilated Jewish backgrounds, arriving in this country before fascism caused many of their peers to flee to Britain and beyond in the late 1930s. They were modernists but without the benefit of association with the seminal Bauhaus design school in Germany, another possible reason for their neglect.

Their stories have been told in scholarly biographies and academic papers. Here they are considered together in the context of their ambitions for and work on high-rise council housing.

The idea for this book came from several seasons spent as a volunteer tour guide for the National Trust at Goldfinger's house at 2 Willow Road in Hampstead. Spending time in the house he designed and built as a young man and where he lived for the rest of his life gives volunteers the feeling (perhaps the illusion?) that we know Ernö and his family well. It gave me the confidence to retell his story in tandem with that of his contemporary and rival, Lubetkin. It may provide useful lessons for resolving our current housing crises, though I leave readers to consider what those lessons might be.

Given my starting point, the people who have

contributed most to this book are the staff and volunteers at 2 Willow Road between 2014 and 2017, from whom I learned a great deal about Goldfinger and his work. Subsequent heritage volunteer roles elsewhere have shown me that volunteering is a powerful stimulus to understanding historic sites and those who lived in them.

Several people were kind enough to read and comment on sections of the text as it evolved, including members of the U3A Creative Writing Group in Bath. Colleagues from Imperial College were also encouraging. The most assiduous commentator was Dr Bob Barker, who read early draft materials, suggesting many corrections and improvements. This has led to a better text and any surviving defects are entirely mine.

## PICTURE CREDITS.

All images by Nicholas Russell apart from:

4. Richard Parmiter, p.15
5. Derek Voller, p.16
19. (C) 1988 Peter Marshall, p.74
29. Will Collin (dOgwalker), p.124
32. Diamond Geezer, p.127

# 1

ERNÖ GOLDFINGER AND BERTHOLD
LUBETKIN. MONSTERS WITH THE BEST OF
INTENTIONS.

People first noticed Ernö Goldfinger (1902–87) as a student in Paris in the 1920s, an opinionated Hungarian, aggressive but attractive to women. He first displayed disruptive tendencies as a teenager in 1918 during a communist putsch in Budapest. The communists were soon overthrown by an anti-Semitic government and, as the Goldfingers were Jewish, only nifty footwork by Ernö's father kept them out of trouble. He registered the family as Polish citizens and moved them to the relative safety of Vienna.

When he arrived in England in the mid-1930s Goldfinger stood out again: a tall, loud, argumentative architect who bullied his staff and thought he was always right. He was a dandy, dressing like an English gentleman in brogues and tweeds, though any illusion was undermined by his thick Hungarian accent. His architectural practice was small but, even so, in 1955 he essentially replaced his staff twice over when he sacked thirteen assistants. He ordered the office to keep all his drawings to allow posterity to appreciate his genius.

The name Goldfinger is embedded in the popular mind, not as a star architect but as a James Bond villain. *Goldfinger* was published in 1959 and filmed in 1964. Ian Fleming chose the name because he disliked the real Goldfinger and his architecture. Fleming's *Goldfinger* was deeply unpleasant and one of Ernö's assistants suggested the fictional character closely resembled the real Ernö.

But he was also an indulgent family man, liberal with his three children and married for more than fifty years to Ursula (née Blackwell). Before the war he designed educational toys and worked closely with the progressive toy retailers, Paul and Marjorie Abbatt. Many of his exasperated assistants recognised how much he taught them and remained grateful. He could be warm and generous, famously with Ursula holding parties over many decades. The pair were also notable collectors of modern art, accumulating some six hundred paintings, drawings and sculptures.

Berthold Lubetkin (1901–90) was a fiercely intelligent, largely self-educated Russian, a youthful member of the communist party in Moscow in 1916. After the Bolshevik revolution in the following year he became a politically engaged art student. His Jewish business family felt insecure under the Soviet regime and migrated *en masse* to Poland, except for Berthold, who stayed in Russia before moving to Germany and then France.

Like Goldfinger, Lubetkin was something of a lothario: confident, energetic and good-looking. He arrived in London in 1931 and with a group of radical young British architects founded the collective practice Tecton. He met his wife, Margaret Church, as a nineteen-year-old intern at Tecton in 1934. She shared his left-wing views, not as a Marxist but from a deep sense of social injustice. The pair married in 1939 and had four children, only three of whom survived. The children were born in Gloucestershire, where the family moved in 1940 when Lubetkin took up a second career in farming.

After the war Lubetkin set his children against each other to compete for his affection and their sibling rivalries lasted into adulthood. His youngest child, Louise, born in 1950, went as a teenager to Germany, where she had an accident that needed surgery. A surgeon undertook the painful operation without anaesthetic. When she came home her parents were unsympathetic. They refused to believe that the surgeon might have been an ex-Nazi who assumed Louise was Jewish and treated her accordingly. They told her the cruel treatment must have been her own fault. At that point Lubetkin took enormous trouble to deny that he had any Jewish connections whatsoever.

Clearly Lubetkin and Goldfinger were deeply flawed, but they shared the virtue of dedication to building the best possible housing for ordinary people. They both believed that city dwellers were best served by high-rise apartment blocks rather than terraced housing or cottage estates in suburbs or the countryside. The latter developments gobbled up land and forced residents to commute back into cities for work and leisure. It was better to try and keep them within the city limits.

They were enthusiasts for reinforced concrete as the best material for building blocks of flats. These were meticulously planned, almost classical in adherence to proportion and harmony, though they never took the extreme modernist line that rational design should drive out feeling. They believed all residents of their apartments should have positive emotional connections to their homes. Despite similarities in background and ambition, they did not get on. Goldfinger said he thought Lubetkin was a scoundrel.

Their chosen architectural form, the high-rise domestic tenement block, was never popular in Britain, and cost-cutting undermined the quality and appearance of many of the slabs and towers that were built. That was not so true of Lubetkin and Goldfinger. They fought cuts and tried to maintain high construction and decorative standards on their estates. Their achievements for the public good were substantial and their stories deserve telling.

## Sources

Allan, J. (1992), *Berthold Lubetkin. Architecture and the Tradition of Progress*, London: RIBA Publications.

Ezard, J. (2005), 'How Goldfinger nearly became Goldprick', *The Guardian*, 3 June.

Kehoe, L. (1995), *In This Dark House, A Memoir*, London: Viking.

National Trust/National Sound Archive, *Passionate Rationalism. Recollections of Ernö Goldfinger*, undated CD.

Obituary (1987), 'Mr Ernö Goldfinger, Advocate of High-rise Building', *The Times*, 16 November, 18.

Sassier, G. (2013), 'Goldfingerism', *The Times*, 19 July, 27.

Short, A. (2013), 'Sacked by Ernö', *The Times*, 13 July, 25.

Warburton, N. (2005), *Ernö Goldfinger – the Life of an Architect*, Abingdon: Routledge.

# 2

THE FINE START AND UNTIMELY END TO
HIGH-RISE COUNCIL HOUSING IN LONDON.

The 25th of July 1946 was a key date for high-rise council housing in Britain. The then-Minister of Health, Aneurin Bevan (whose remit included housing), crossed the urban wastes of post-war London to visit one of the city's poorest boroughs, Finsbury. Before the war that borough had been a crowded patchwork of run-down Victorian terraces, many occupied by several families, most living in squalor. Existing houses had been bomb-damaged and most demolished. Only two short terraces were retained and refurbished on the site he was visiting.

Bevan had been invited to lay the foundation stone for the Spa Green Estate. This was to have unheard-of levels of luxury for council housing. The estate was finished in 1950, delayed by shortages of material and labour. There were three slab blocks of flats, two eight storeys high (Tunbridge House and Wells House) with a third, sinuous block, of five storeys (Sadler House). High-rise is conventionally defined as buildings over six storeys, so there were two high-rise blocks here. The estate had 129 flats at a density of two hundred people per acre, higher than the recommended figure for London overall, but perfectly comfortable in these buildings at this location.

Spa Green was well built, its elevations brick- and tile-faced. The flats were large with excellent facilities, including lifts and fitted kitchens, surrounded by landscaped gardens. There was good transport in and out of the city centre. The blocks ran north to south so the flats faced east and west with good morning and afternoon light. The bedrooms on the two parallel high-rise blocks faced the quiet open space between them. Most flats had private balconies to give some personal outdoor space and residents also had access to communal gardens.

The estate was designed by the Tecton Group, led by Berthold Lubetkin. Spa Green was, and remains, a desirable place to live. This is partly because Tecton were leaders in using reinforced concrete, which allows design flexibility, permitting better interior layouts with a focus on light and ventilation. In the following decades, as costs and corners were repeatedly cut, Lubetkin could never equal the quality of Spa Green with later council designs. Spa Green was among the first of several progressive council housing schemes in inner London planned before the war but only built afterwards. None were as self-consciously modernist or well built as Spa Green.

Nearly twenty years after Spa Green was finished, in 1968, one of London's most iconic council towers was completed, the twenty-seven-storey Balfron Tower on the Brownfield Estate in Poplar. At the time it was the tallest residential tower in Europe. High-rise council housing had accelerated through the 1950s and '60s but people were beginning to doubt the wisdom of building this way. Ernö Goldfinger designed Balfron and lived in a flat near the top of the tower for two months with Ursula so they could see for themselves what high-rise living was like and quiz new occupants about their feelings. Goldfinger knew there was a groundswell against high-rise and was anxious to counter what he considered inaccurate prejudice. His observations and interviews were positive and he left the flat confident he could rebut most of the arguments against tower blocks.

Critics argued that the Goldfingers' stay was just a public-relations stunt. That is unfair; Goldfinger used the feedback to change the design of the second giant residential tower he was working on, Trellick Tower in North Kensington. Most significantly he installed three lifts at Trellick; the two in Balfron were clearly inadequate. He also ensured that the access corridors in Trellick were heated, a decision that later came back to haunt him.

The Goldfingers left Balfron and went home to Hampstead on the 16th of May, the very same day that a twenty-two-storey residential tower at Canning Town in Newham partially collapsed, killing four people and seriously injuring seventeen more. The event undermined Goldfinger's confidence, though in the end he was satisfied that there was nothing wrong with his tower. It was not going to fall down.

Ronan Point was built with the Scandinavian Larson Nielsen Large Panel System (LPS). This system had only been safety-tested for buildings up to six storeys high but was used for much taller blocks. By 1968 thirty thousand flats had been built in Britain using LPS in slab and tower blocks over six storeys high. Ronan Point had inadequate steel bolts holding the panels together which began rusting straight away. Many voids that should have been filled with concrete or mortar were stuffed with newspaper.

The *coup de grace* was the substandard gas supply, the cause of a kitchen explosion on the eighteenth floor that triggered the collapse. Ronan Point was refurbished and reoccupied, and many people still liked living there, but even with an upgrade the tower was unsound. It was demolished in 1986, the rubble used as hardcore under London City Airport. Despite its reprieve the original collapse of Ronan Point was a watershed – public trust in high-rise building was fatally undermined.

Investigation of tower blocks following this saga revealed widespread bad design and poor planning, together with slipshod building control that allowed far too many substandard high-rise buildings to go up. These issues have continued to undermine high-rise blocks. The Grenfell Tower fire of June 2017 triggered another major inquiry and national survey into the state of the country's high-rise housing stock, mainly built by the private sector or housing associations after the demise of council building in the early 1980s. The survey revealed a horrific picture of low standards and neglect. The sins of a greedy and incompetent public sector in the 1960s and '70s have been repeated by a greedy and incompetent private sector in the twenty-first century.

Back in the earlier era, Goldfinger carried on with Trellick Tower and the rest of the Cheltenham Estate in Ladbroke Grove. The thirty-one-storey Trellick was finished in 1972 and he briefly had the tallest residential building in Europe again. As at Balfron, the first tenants loved it. By the mid-1970s things had gone downhill and the media called Trellick the 'Tower of Terror'. Their stories of social problems were exaggerated but Goldfinger still found himself the last man standing against the deluge of criticism, satirised in 1975 by J.G. Ballard's novel, *High Rise*, the tale of a dystopian forty-storey tower block where the residents are driven mad by the building itself with the architect who designed it living in a penthouse on the top floor.

So while Lubetkin was responsible for the first and perhaps the best middle- to high-rise council estate ever built, Goldfinger is always associated with the last, apparently disastrous, council high-rise towers to go up. Between them they began and ended the twentieth-century boom in high-rise council housing. Political and social circumstances, and changing architectural tastes, undermined much of what they (and others like them) were trying to achieve.

## Sources

Allan, J. (1992), *Berthold Lubetkin. Architecture and the Tradition of Progress*, London: RIBA Publications.

Booth, R. (2022), 'Will the industry ever stop passing the buck over building safety scandal?', and '"I don't sleep well" Life in a worthless "flammable" flat', *The Guardian*, 11 January, 15, two of many newspaper reports on slow government response after the Grenfell fire disaster.

Carr, H. (2013), 'Utopias, Dystopias and the Changing Lawscapes of Social Housing: A Case Study of the Spa Green Estate London UK', *Australian Feminist Law Journal*, **38**, 109–127.

localhistory.co.uk., 'The Lubetkin and Tecton Design for Spa Road Flats', accessed 29.03.2021.

Roberts, D. (2015), *Balfron Tower, a Building Archive*, Ernö and Ursula Goldfinger, 1968, and Oldham, R. (2010), 'Ursula Goldfinger's Balfron Tower Diary and Notes', courtesy of the Twentieth Century Society, accessed 19.03.2021.

UK Housing Wiki, Tower block, accessed 30.03.2021.

Warburton, N. (2005), *Ernö Goldfinger – the Life of an Architect*, Abingdon: Routledge.

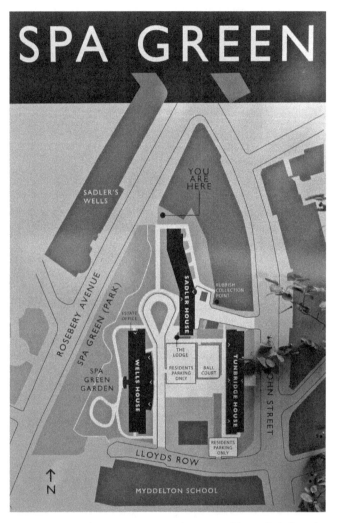

1. On-site map of Spa Green Estate, Finsbury. A small but perfectly formed
park city or urban village.

*2. Wells House front facade with main entrance and parabolic cover,
Spa Green Estate, Finsbury.*

*3. Wells House rear facade, Spa Green Estate, Finsbury.*

*4. Balfron Tower and Carradale House, Brownfield Estate, Tower Hamlets.*

*5. The Collapse of Ronan Point, Canning Town.*

# 3

WHAT DID RESIDENTS OF HIGH-RISE
COUNCIL HOUSING THINK OF WHERE
THEY LIVED?

## Post-War Council Housing

After the Second World War, Britain's long-term housing shortage was worse than ever. To begin with local authorities, supported by a Labour government, built high quality yet affordable homes for rent, a combination that presented an insoluble long-term paradox. No political economy has been able to provide good housing for everyone. Conservative administrations undermined public housing quality from the 1950s, insisting that most people should own their own homes, developed by the private sector and funded with mortgages.

But initially there was idealism and high-quality council housing was built for anybody who wanted to rent it. Council schemes were for 'general needs'; social class mixing was encouraged. At the start there was little emphasis on high-rise tenements, but living in a modern city is only feasible if there are plenty of high- and middle-rise apartment blocks. Such blocks have never been fully accepted in Britain, so there also had to be significant growth in sprawling low-rise suburbs and remote satellite towns.

Alternating Labour and Conservative governments competed to build the maximum number of new homes. The peak was in 1953 when over 318,000 units were built, more than two hundred thousand of them council homes. To increase the volume and speed of construction, building standards were reduced while a 1954 Housing Act stopped councils building socially mixed estates. They had to focus on redevelopment following slum clearance. As a result council accommodation began a slow decline towards poor-quality transient housing for the least well-off people. Multi-storey blocks were more expensive than terraced housing and to redress this difference, there was bigger government subsidy for high-rise construction. The result was an increase in high-rise building, not just in city centres but sometimes inappropriately on distant cottage estates.

Some local councils were almost Soviet in their housing allocation and too many tower-block facades were exposed concrete, *concrete brut*. Both factors further contributed to the dislike of high-rise in Britain.

Lubetkin and Goldfinger were not guilty; they either avoided raw concrete facades or worked hard to make them visually interesting. Nor did they want to dictate to tenants how they should live. If high-rise council blocks with landscaped communal green space and access to urban facilities had been well planned and built between the 1950s and '70s, the towers might have better survived the unemployment and poverty that followed British de-industrialisation in the 1980s. All types of public housing suffered, but physical and social decay in high-rise estates was more obvious. Neglect of buildings and loss of well-paid jobs were the major causes of the decline in such developments. It was certainly not all the fault of architects and planners.

## Living in the Sky

Once upon a time I lived near the Corporation of London's Barbican, essentially a posh council estate. This area had been a confusion of terraces and workshops before it was wiped out by German bombing. Reconstruction began in 1952 with the Golden Lane Estate, designed for workers servicing the offices of London's financial centre. In the late 1950s the Corporation began planning an estate to attract middle-class professionals to live near their work. At a time when inner London was a mass of bombsites this was a hard sell. The new estate had to be high quality with first-rate facilities. The designers of the Golden Lane Estate, Chamberlain, Powell and Bon, were commissioned for the Barbican and came up with a brutalist park city.

The project was huge and beset with problems throughout. It was begun in the early 1960s but not finished until 1982. In the end it has proved a success. Given the right circumstances it shows that a brutalist, urban, high- and middle-rise residential park city can work. It needs good funding, long-term maintenance, a high level of security and residents committed to keeping up standards. If any of these factors are missing, high-rise estates work less well, though they are seldom the dystopias of popular imagination. The key issue is cost. Council housing of any type has to resolve Bevan's original dilemma of combining quality with economy. The Barbican is a special case. There was no attempt at social mixing. It was (and remains) an estate for the middle class, who can afford to pay for quality.

The estate is a mixture of flats and houses, partially set in parkland, served with leisure and social facilities, free of motor traffic and well connected to the city centre by public transport. While few estates have achieved the comfort of the Barbican, is it possible that people living in less salubrious high-rise estates were (and are) reasonably happy? How do residents actually feel about living in high-rise towers?

A long-term study of people relocated to high-rise flats in Glasgow in the 1960s and '70s concluded there was no general conclusion; some people settled, some did not, some liked it, some did not, while for many it was not a life-changing event. This picture of mixed reactions was echoed in Tony Parker's 1980s oral history of the Brandon Estate in Southwark. This was begun in the 1950s, a socially mixed estate of working- and middle-class residents, living in a combination of tower blocks, middle-rise slabs, three-storey blocks and refurbished terraces. Parker interviewed people across the whole estate and found a range of feelings about living there, ranging from despair to elation. There was a persistent undertow of distress at physical decay, lack of supervision, invasion by squatters and criminals, and widespread lease-breaking by residents working from home. Their premises were repurposed for activities running from factory production to brothel-keeping.

Residents on Glasgow's notorious Red Road flats had generally negative feelings about their estate, and its unloved multiple towers were demolished in 2013 and 2015. These had housed nearly five thousand people and, although only two miles from the city centre, always felt remote. By the 1990s they had accumulated baggage of violent crime and suicides. At the beginning people were happy and even at the end some residents spoke up for life on the estate, although seeds of decay had been there from the start. Jephcott undertook extensive social research on the Red Road towers in the late 1960s and found there were no play facilities for the many families with small children. The estate was supplied by expensive mobile vans; there was only one small shop. There were no doctors, no dentists and poor transport links. Failure to provide such essential infrastructure was endlessly repeated.

A worldwide meta-review of high-rise living showed a range of responses to life in the sky. In general residents of low-rise were more satisfied than those in high-rise, especially families with young children. High-rise residents had fewer friends and helped each other less. Satisfaction with high-rise living went up in more expensive towers in better neighbourhoods. They could be positively attractive, as the Barbican demonstrated.

The overall conclusion must be that high-rise living of itself is not the main cause of dissatisfaction, except perhaps for families with young children. It is also clear that blocks set in attractive sites and properly managed can be decent places to live. Goldfinger and Lubetkin always argued that the main problems with high-rise were poor build quality (for which they must take some responsibility), high rents, neglect of social planning, poor maintenance, inadequate security and unpleasant surroundings. Architects had little control over the last five phenomena.

Goldfinger's Trellick Tower on the Cheltenham Estate in North Kensington became the poster child for what had gone wrong. Council estates had become centres of deprivation because too many tenants were on low income or unemployed and looked out over industrial and domestic wastelands. All the communal parts of Trellick Tower, the 'streets in the sky', were heated (because tenants in Balfron had complained about the unheated corridors), and since they were open to the public became magnets for vagrants and the homeless, who intimidated residents. There was vandalism, drug-dealing, mugging and prostitution, though their extent was probably exaggerated. The pressures drove many tenants out.

In the 1970s Goldfinger could not persuade the Greater London Council (GLC) to invest in security, landscaping or other environmental improvements. Poor maintenance made the situation worse. Conventional 'wisdom' put the blame on the buildings, not poverty and neglect among the residents. Even the distinguished journalist Simon Jenkins could claim in an article about East London in *The Times* in 2000, 'Poverty is not Poplar's curse. The curse is architecture' (quoted in Roberts, p143).

Bad housing at too high a price for many people remains the norm two decades into the twenty-first century. Arguments about the role of high-rise blocks rumble on. In 2013 the Think Tank Policy Exchange confirmed the unpopularity of tower blocks and blamed architects and planners, fair and square. It called for the demolition of all towers. Its surveys showed people disliked flats, especially when they were in tower blocks. The most favoured type of home was a bungalow, the form with the lowest housing density of all. To be fair to Policy Exchange, they did not favour inner-city bungalows but proposed reviving dense terraced housing at 'proper, human scale'. This can certainly work if it is carefully done, as in the London Borough of Camden and elsewhere during the 1960s.

In defiance of ongoing pressures to demolish tower blocks, some residents continue to support them. The drab Seven Sisters estate in Rochdale is a case in point. It was originally built, like the Barbican, to attract professional people to the city centre. Build quality was good and rents were high. Nevertheless the same fate befell this estate as so many others. The place is no paradise, there are the usual problems with drug-dealing and mugging, there are lots of graffiti and the lift shafts no doubt smell of urine, but many residents blame an uncaring society. They see the down-and-outs as victims not perpetrators. They want to stay in their large flats with reasonable rents, good views and easy access to the town's facilities.

Goldfinger's apparent disasters have been re-evaluated. John Grindrod visited Balfron Tower several times in the 2000s. Tower Hamlets Council transferred ownership of Balfron and the rest of the Brownfield Estate to Poplar Harca Housing Association in 2007. The association planned to sell the flats in Balfron Tower to fund the refurbishment of the rest of the estate for social rent. In the noughties the association rented some Balfron flats to artists and John Grindrod met Katherine Hibbert there, more than forty years after the tower was built. She had a spacious, high-level, two-bedroom flat for herself, her boyfriend and her cat. It was bigger than flats she had rented in the private sector but cramped for a family of four who might have been typical council occupants. Residents were generally friendly and helpful, long-term council tenants rather than the transient populations of many private developments. The views were fabulous over much of London and Katherine liked the building, both inside and out.

By around 2017 all existing tenants had been decanted from Balfron and refurbishment began. None of the 130 flats are to be available for social rent; they will be sold to private buyers from the summer of 2022. There were over a thousand expressions of interest before the flats were released for sale. A few have been restored to their original appearance, but most interiors have been stripped of internal walls to create open-plan spaces with contemporary fixtures. The internal common parts have been restored to their original pattern, but the facades of white-painted wooden window frames have been replaced by bands of anodised aluminium, totally altering the external appearance. So while there has been desecration the tower is once more composed of desirable flats. Unfortunately they are for sale to affluent professionals rather than providing a mix of owned and rented homes for a range of social classes.

When the redevelopment was being planned there was some academic analysis of the roots of the dystopia at the tower. This revealed not only the effects of social decay but also a cultural association between Goldfinger's personality and the reputation of his buildings: a nasty man had built nasty homes. This was an unjustified smear on a communist idealist. Current and past residents took part in workshops and interviews to explore what they really felt about living in Balfron Tower. Some were initially intimidated by the tower but eventually liked it. They appreciated the spacious interiors, the attention to design detail and general build quality (especially the sound insulation between flats), the light, and the dramatic views from the large windows. They noted the deterioration in the original social cohesion and lack of maintenance, though installation of a door-entry system had restored some security. The 'street' layout had encouraged some social interaction, just as Goldfinger had originally intended.

Post-Ronan Point, tower-block building was reined back. The increase in subsidy with height (started in 1958) was abandoned in 1967. Some of the worst towers have since been demolished. The more astute residents knew the buildings were not to blame. It was the lack of maintenance and the people who were forced to live in them. Handled and managed better, high-rise council estates could have been a good long-term solution to the problems of housing people at high density in cities. Given the political will it would make sense to try again. In the 1990s the late Richard Rogers revived the idea that dense, high-rise urban housing had major benefits, but his vision was only partially realised. Like the left-wing politicians and architects of the mid-twentieth century, he advocated good housing for everyone but found the economic circle impossible to square. His practice wound up designing luxury apartments for affluent buyers.

## Sources

Barnett, D. (2016), 'Modernist dream: dystopian nightmare: the ups and downs of tower blocks', *The Independent*, accessed 21.03.2021.

Boys Smith, N. and Morton, A. (2013), 'Create Streets, not just multi-storey estates', Policy Exchange and CREATE streets, accessed 12.03.2021.

Braghieri, N. (2019), 'The Towers of Terror: A Critical Analysis of

Ernö Goldfinger's Balfron and Trellick Towers', *Urban Planning*, **4**, 223–249.

Broughton, J. (2018), *Municipal Dreams. The Rise and Fall of Council Housing*, London: Verso.

Gifford, R. (2007), 'The consequences of living in high-rise buildings', *Architectural Science Review*, **50**, 2–17.

Glendinning, M. and Muthesius, S. (1994), *Tower Block: Modern Public Housing in England, Scotland, Wales and Northern Ireland*, New Haven and London: Yale University Press.

Grindrod, J. (2013), *Concretopia. A Journey Around the Rebuilding of Postwar Britain*, Brecon: Old Street Publishing.

Hanley, L. (2017), *Estates. An Intimate History*, London: Granta (first published 2007).

Herrman, J. (January 2021), 'Towers on the Hill: the dwindling life of Rochdale's "Seven Sisters"', *The Mill*, accessed 12.03.2021.

Hill, A. (2003), 'Council estate decline spawns new underclass', *The Observer*, accessed as Housing, *The Guardian*, accessed 21.10.2020.

Kearns, A., Wright, V., Abrams, L., and Hazley, B. (2019), 'Slum Clearance and relocation: a reassessment of social outcomes combining short-term and long-term perspectives', *Housing Studies*, **34**, 201–225.

Municipal Housing, J. Broughton's Blog (2015), 'The Brandon Estate, Southwark II: "It was going to be paradise"', accessed 05.01.2022.

Parker, A. (1996), *The People of Providence. A Housing Estate and Some of Its Inhabitants*, London: Eland (first published Hutchinson, 1983).

Roberts, D. (2017), Chapter 8 '"We felt magnificent being up there" – Ernö Goldfinger's Balfron Tower and the Campaign to Keep It Public', in Guillery, Peter and Kroll, David (Eds), *Learning from London's Past*, London: RIBA Publishing.

University of the West of England, 'The History of Council Housing', http://fet.uwe.ac.uk/conweb/house_ages/council_housing/print.htm, accessed 18.06.2020.

Wainwright, O. (2021), 'Obituary. Lord Rogers of Riverside. One of the greats of British architecture who ushered in a new era for the inner city', *The Guardian*, Journal Section, 20 December, 6/7.

Wainwright, O. (2022), 'I love living there – it was a complete cross-section of society', *The Guardian*, G2 Section, 26 July, 6/7.

Wilkinson, D. (2017), 'What's life like in a Greater Manchester Tower Block?', *Manchester Evening News*, accessed 12.03.2021.

Wright, V. (2015), 'Red Road and Pearl Jephcott's "Homes in High Flats"', *Housing and Wellbeing in Glasgow*, accessed 16.03.2021.

*6. The Barbican Estate, London. High- and middle-rise apartment blocks.*

*7. The Barbican Estate, London. Social and cultural facilities.*

*8. Trellick Tower with the ends of low-rise terraced housing, Cheltenham Estate, North Kensington, viewed from a speeding GWR train on tracks running close to the estate.*

*9. Site plan of the Brownfield Estate, Tower Hamlets. The footprints of Balfron Tower and Carradale House to the left overlooking the Blackwall Tunnel approach road are very small, allowing extensive open space on this city estate.*

*10. Balfron Tower rising over low-rise terracing on the Brownfield Estate. Its new livery is brown anodised aluminium.*

*11. Sales placard for Balfron Tower flats, 2022.*

# 4

<hr>

## MODERNISM AND REINFORCED CONCRETE, PARIS 1926. LUBETKIN AND GOLDFINGER AT AUGUSTE PERRET'S TRAINING STUDIO.

L ubetkin and Goldfinger crossed paths for the first time in Paris in 1926 at the training studio run by Auguste Perret. Architectural students attended such studios to gain experience of professional work. Goldfinger was a diploma student at the École Nationale Superiore des Beaux-Arts, while Lubetkin was an occasional student at the École Speciale d'Architecture. How did they both wind up in Perret's studio?

Goldfinger enrolled at the École Nationale Superiore des Beaux-Arts in 1922. He had decided to become an architect in 1916 after his father bought an old house in

Budapest and commissioned a local architect to refurbish it. He was thrilled by the drawings of as-yet-unrealised three-dimensional buildings. He found architectural plans beautiful.

His Beaux-Arts diploma should have taken six years, but he spun it out over ten, graduating in 1932 when he was nearly thirty. The delay was partly a result of attending Perret's studio. The modernist diploma project he began there in 1926 was not accepted by the conservative faculty at the Beaux-Arts. He had to wait for them to catch up and they eventually accepted his work.

Lubetkin came to Paris in 1925. As an art student in Moscow he had been immersed in the visual art trends of Soviet Russia, abstraction and constructivism. He preferred the utilitarian expression of the latter – applying art directly to industry, although in the short term he explored a range of revolutionary artistic expression. He left Moscow in 1921 after government clampdown on cultural freedom. He valued freedom of expression above all else and would not tolerate restriction. It drove him to Berlin, where he worked as a translator for an exhibition of Soviet art. He managed to stay on, supporting himself with further translation work.

By 1923 he had settled on architecture as a career and enrolled at two institutions, the Berlin Textile Academy and the School of Building at Charlottenburg, where he came across reinforced concrete and began to enthuse about it. In 1924 he decamped to Warsaw, where most of his family then lived. He enrolled at the Warsaw Polytechnic but found the architecture course too conventional. He needed somewhere more exciting. Paris was the obvious answer. He spent much of 1925 and '26 in that city and built himself a one-man education programme at various institutions.

Perret was asked to run a training studio by a cohort of Beaux-Arts students who had read Le Corbusier's revolutionary textbook *Vers Une Architecture* in 1923, full of the modernist ideas being developed across Continental Europe. The students knew Le Corbusier lived in Paris and, assuming he had an architectural practice, asked him to set up a studio for them. Le Corbusier declined but made a suggestion. He had learned much of his architectural thinking from Auguste Perret, when he had worked for him before the First World War. Why not ask Perret to set up a studio? Perret was flattered and agreed, though since he had never finished his own Beaux-Arts diploma there were problems with the plan. Goldfinger, especially, imbibed Perret's enthusiasm for reinforced concrete.

Lubetkin attended Perret's studio from the École Speciale d'Architecture. In contrast to the meticulous Goldfinger, Lubetkin was scruffy and unreliable, but Perret liked him and tolerated his irregular attendance. Lubetkin and Goldfinger shared a gift for charming potential mentors, which they used ruthlessly to further their careers. Lubetkin arrived at the studio as an occasional student because he had been thrown out of the École Speciale for his iconoclastic response to a student assignment for a war memorial. He produced a shocking proposal. A vast cylindrical, gun barrel-like tank filled with a huge volume of red fluid to represent the blood spilled in the war. His scheme was a memorial to pointless carnage rather than patriotic sacrifice. The idea did not go down well at the École Speciale but probably appealed to Goldfinger, although not enough to persuade him to like its creator. The pair took against each other from the start.

Lubetkin picked up the strong constructivist attitudes in Perret's work. He designed buildings with an understanding of how they were to be built. Perret also concerned himself with minor details like doorknobs and light switches. Lubetkin and Goldfinger were lucky to work with Perret, who was a modernist before the term was invented. The short associations were critical to their professional development.

Perret (1874–1954) was a pioneer of steel-reinforced concrete, a relatively new material in the early twentieth century: strong, flexible and often cheaper than timber, steel, brick or stone. Despite its unpromising look and feel, it could also be exposed as a decorative finish. Some examples of Perret's early work can be seen in Paris, notably the Rue Franklin apartments, designed and built by Perret Frères between 1902 and 1904. This block is an early example of the domestic use of reinforced concrete. The floors and columns are structural; none of the external or internal walls are load bearing. While Perret designed identical apartment layouts on each floor, later occupants could (if they wished) remove the walls to make an open-plan space or put new dividing walls wherever they liked. The concrete framework gave this design freedom, its leading benefit for domestic modernism. Perret faced the building with elaborate, decorated tile work and broke the facade up with vertical re-entrants and angled balconies. The overall effect is somewhat fussy.

Not far away is the Théâtre des Champs-Élysées, built between 1911 and 1913 largely to Perret's designs. Once again a reinforced concrete frame is the key feature that allows auditoria and foyers to be large and open, maximising circulation space and giving uninterrupted sight lines from all seats to the stages. The exterior walls are faced with pale grey stone, the surface broken with restrained pilasters. The finish is more austere than the elaborate Art Nouveau style popular at the time. This austerity hints at modernism to come, where surface decoration was minimised and the aesthetics of a building depend on the harmony and proportions of the enclosed spaces, wall surfaces, and careful shaping and positioning of doors and windows.

Perret had introduced Le Corbusier to reinforced concrete, which the latter began to use before the First World War as he put together ideas for *Vers Une Architecture.* In that book he argued that architecture was stuck in the past and asked why architecture could not rival the progress made in engineering with motor cars, aeroplanes and ocean liners.

During the First World War, with an engineer friend, Le Corbusier patented a method for building temporary reinforced concrete houses ('*Maisons Dom-Ino*'), assemblies of three slabs and six columns of concrete, into which any arrangement of rooms could be fitted. The units were flexible because the structural work was placed on the framework of columns, slab floors and a slab roof. Internal and external walls could then be made of any material and put in any position.

The simplest way to 'dress' such a frame was with thin concrete external walls with big windows to maximise interior light together with a waterproof layer of asphalt on the top slab to form a roof. The walls were often painted white. Thin concrete had poor sound and thermal insulation, and flat roofs often leaked. Early modernists did not properly understand how to use the new materials that enthralled them.

One of Le Corbusier's early post-war commissions was the Villa La Roche completed in 1925 for the art collector Raoul La Roche. It is now the Le Corbusier museum. The house has a reinforced concrete frame, faced in white-painted concrete, partly built on slender pillars, piloti, with flat roofs and sun terracing. It is an early example of the modernist style popular in the late 1920s and 1930s, white concrete cubes or cuboids arranged in angular association. Such white boxes were never to Goldfinger's taste; he referred to them contemptuously as 'Casbah' architecture.

Le Corbusier (and the other modernist pioneers) advocated architecture of pure geometry. He modified the classical aesthetics of antiquity, expressed in buildings like the Parthenon, a key illustration in *Vers Une Architecture* shown cheek by jowl with American grain silos, whose aesthetic lay in how form reflected function. Neither building had much distracting external decoration.

Le Corbusier explored the architectural writing of the Roman engineer Vitruvius and the Renaissance architectural thought of Leonardo da Vinci and Leon Battista Alberti, and came up with his own system of aesthetic proportion, which he called the 'modulor'. He published two books on the scheme, *Modulor* (1948) and *Modulor 2* (1955). His motivation was the incompatibility between imperial feet and inches and the metric system. The latter had the virtue of rationality but made no reference to the natural scale of the human body.

Le Corbusier believed modulor relationships based, like Leonardo's *Vitruvian Man*, on the relative proportions of parts of the human body, would generate harmony and proportion in his buildings. For instance he used them to design the *Unité d'Habitation* housing project in Marseilles in the 1940s and the later Berlin *Unité d'Habitation*. As a close student of Le Corbusier, Lubetkin must have known the modulor system. It is not clear whether he also used a consistent system for working out dimensions and proportions or used judgements based on experience with individual projects. He did not follow Le Corbusier's later style of facing his buildings in unpainted raw concrete; Lubetkin's facades were usually covered in decorative patterns. He abandoned Le Corbusier's earlier signature white paint on concrete before the master gave it up himself.

Goldfinger said little about his use of geometry in design. He made extensive use of a set of rectangles derived from a square by adding fragments determined by classical geometric proportions, ratios such as 1:√2, 2:3 (a square and a half), the double square, 2:1 and the Golden Mean 1:1.618. Apart from the double square, all these rectangles are similar, but Goldfinger claimed they had different and conflicting properties, which meant they should not be mixed. With interior designs, even where the given space dimensions were not to his choosing, he managed to manipulate the spaces to conform to his preferred ratios. The facade of his house at 2 Willow Road is a perfect square, the depth a double square, and window positions, sizes and room heights also conform to his conventions.

Soon after the war he standardised all his designs on a planning grid of 2'9". This dimension was derived from a standard door width of 2'6" plus frame, a reference to both a fundamental feature of a house and its dependence on the size of a human. Goldfinger used the human body as a source of *scale* rather than proportion. He owed to Vitruvius the central place of the square with resultant harmonious rectangles. His near Golden Section grid of 16'6" x 10'1" was a design denominator he used all the way from small domestic kitchens up to multi-thousand square foot sets of high-rise office and residential blocks. All Modernists used classical geometry and Renaissance architectural practice as the basis of their aesthetic decisions, but in subtly different ways.

We are running ahead. A year before *Vers une Architecture* came out, in 1922, Le Corbusier presented a radical plan for a *Ville Contemporine* at a Paris exhibition, a fantasy city for up to three million people to live in sixty-storey apartment towers surrounded by lower-rise, zigzag blocks, set in landscaped parkland. The scheme was not entirely original; Perret had earlier imagined a similar city. Le Corbusier's towers were raised on columns (piloti), to save on foundation costs and allow roads and other services to be separated from living spaces and circulating people. He argued that piloti would let people see 'through' the buildings and create the impression that they were floating. Concrete frames allowed such tall structures to be built encased with lightweight, non-load-bearing walls.

Le Corbusier and Perret, and later Lubetkin and Goldfinger among others, championed the skyscraper park city as an ideal solution to urban domestic living and the ghost of this idea haunted the post-war rebuilding of British cities with high-rise council blocks.

## Sources

Allan, J. (1992), *Berthold Lubetkin. Architecture and the Tradition of Progress*, London: RIBA Publications.

Boyd-Bent, J., 'Harmony and Proportion,' About Scotland Arts pages, accessed 08.09.2021.

Braghieri, N. (2019), 'The Tower of Terror: A critical analysis of Ernö Goldfinger's Balfron and Trellick Towers', *Urban Planning*, **4**, 223–249.

Cartwright, M. (n/d), 'Leon Battista Alberti', *World History Encyclopaedia*, accessed 09.09.2021.

Dunnett, J. (1983), 'Ernö Goldfinger. The architect as Constructor', *Architectural Review*, **173**, 42–46.

Dunnett, J. and Hiscock, N., '"To this measure of man": Proportional design in the work of Ernö Goldfinger', pp57–87 in Campbell, L. (2000), *Twentieth-Century Architecture and Its Histories*, The Society of Architectural Historians of Great Britain.

Fletcher, R. (2000), 'Golden Proportions in a Great House: Palladio's Villa Emo', *Nexus Network Journal*, **2**, accessed 08.09.2021.

Le Corbusier (1989), *Towards a New Architecture* (translated from the 13th French Edition by John Rodker with introduction by Frederick Etchells), London: Butterworth Heinemann (originally published in French in 1923).

National Trust/National Sound Archive CD, *Passionate Rationalism. Recollections of Ernö Goldfinger*, undated CD.

Warburton, N. (2005), *Ernö Goldfinger – the Life of an Architect*, Abingdon: Routledge.

*12. Rue Franklin Apartments, Paris, Perret Frères.*

*13. Théâtre des Champs-Élysées, Paris, Auguste Perret.*

*14. Villa La Roche, Paris, Le Corbusier.*

# 5

PREPARATION. LUBETKIN AND
GOLDFINGER BEFORE THE SECOND
WORLD WAR.

TALKING TO THE ANIMALS, THINKING
ABOUT PEOPLE.

In 1926 Lubetkin was still a student in Paris. He refused to take formal exams and without qualifications found it difficult to obtain work. He was given one commission, a nine-storey apartment block at 25 Avenue de Versailles in Paris, built in the Le Corbusier style of white finished concrete and completed in 1931. Otherwise he took on interior and Soviet trade mission design projects and entered architectural competitions for workers' housing in Russia. He refused to go back, nothing could overcome his dislike of Soviet bureaucracy.

He was restless in Paris. In 1929 he visited England and wondered if he might work there. He found out when he befriended three young English visitors to Paris in 1931, one of whom, Godfrey Samuel, was an Oxford graduate with an architectural diploma. Samuel was one of a small group of young enthusiasts for European modernism who wanted to introduce the style to England. Samuel and Lubetkin got on well and hatched a plot for Lubetkin to come to England to design a house for another of the three visitors. Lubetkin came to London on the vague promise of this commission.

The project came to nothing but he stayed on. England was damper, colder and more individualistic than he had imagined with a distrust of modern art and architecture. He found the country culturally narrow-minded and saw himself as a source of fresh thinking. As a real Russian communist walking the streets of London he was in demand for news and commentary on the Soviet Union. He overestimated the ability of his small group of socialist friends to shift British political thought to the left. His dreams of following the Soviet model of building extensive high-rise housing for British workers did not happen.

With no architectural work Lubetkin was poor in the months after he arrived in England. Fortunately Godfrey Samuel kept in touch. He and his newly qualified architect friends could find no work either. One evening in 1932 in a Fitzrovia pub they decided to bring Lubetkin into their loop. Not only was he trained in European modernism, he had already designed and built a block of flats. They invited him to dinner in a Hampstead restaurant. The home contingent was headed by Samuel who brought along Anthony Chitty, Lindsey Drake, Michael Dugdale, Valentine Harding and Francis Skinner. Details are hazy, but the outcome was that Lubetkin and the six young Englishmen formed an unlikely partnership to look for modernist commissions. They used the generic name 'Tecton' for their practice, shorthand for 'Architecton', the ancient Greek word for architecture.

Tecton was to be a collective and seek socially useful work. The strange combination of a close-knit group of English lefties and a Bolshevik alien made a kind of sense. All income was to be equally shared, no matter who acquired a commission or did the design work. In practice this soon broke down, with a bigger slice going to the project leader, usually Lubetkin. Following the modernist creed that buildings should be carefully designed for their function, Lubetkin insisted on close interaction with clients to discover exactly what they needed, followed by intensive research into possible solutions to these needs, 'interrogating the brief'. Several possibilities would be explored. Tecton presented fully worked-up plans of all the options to their clients and explained why the one they proposed was the best. To begin with Tecton had few commissions while the practice did prodigious amounts of work on projects that were never realised. This way of working did not suit all Lubetkin's associates. They were a commune of non-team players and by 1936 most of the original partners had drifted away.

Their first year, 1932, proved especially barren until saved by commissions for animal houses at London Zoo – a new Gorilla House and the Penguin Pond. Tecton designed these buildings for the needs of their occupants and thoroughly investigated the ecology and behaviour of gorillas and penguins as they were understood at the time. These commissions came through Godfrey Samuel. At first Lubetkin's partners were suspicious. It seemed bizarre to design enclosures for animals, but it was ultimately justified by their success.

Lubetkin brought a strong vision of modernism to these enclosures. The designs were based on simple geometry (a circular tube for the Gorilla House, an oval for the Pond). They were built with undisguised reinforced concrete. While the enclosures were partly designed for the needs of the animals, these did not determine their primary form. The tube and oval were used to best display the animals to the public. The forms were not pure, the Gorilla House had porch-ways to draw visitors in and the inner wall of the Penguin Pond had irregular features, some to appeal to penguins, others to visitors. Lubetkin brought in Soviet-design thinking. The daring, unsupported, spiral arrangement of ultra-thin ramps over the Penguin Pond owed a great deal to artistic practice after the Bolshevik revolution. The spiral symbolised its forward progress in structures like Tatlin's proposed giant tower, Rodchenko's three-dimensional constructions, and in his set designs for the Meyerhold Theatre.

Another result of the zoo commissions was Lubetkin's partnership with the Danish structural engineer Ove

Arup. While Lubetkin was keen to work with reinforced concrete he lacked the expertise to use it confidently. He needed a structural engineer who understood it. Arup and Lubetkin quickly struck up a friendship based on shared interests in art, music and philosophy together with a strong desire to build good homes for ordinary people. Arup wanted to move reinforced concrete construction away from column and beam (a hangover from building with steel and wood) to a panel and slab technique. But London County Council (LCC) building regulations forbade the use of load-bearing concrete panels. That did not stop Lubetkin and Arup. They persuaded LCC Building Surveyors that the animal enclosures were temporary and therefore exempt from the regulations.

The most eye-catching elements of Tecton's Penguin Pond were the overlapping walkways, cantilevered over the pool. The calculations for their form, the positions of the reinforcing steels and of the concealed buttresses at the ends were difficult and entirely the work of Arup's small engineering team, notably Felix Samuily. The beauty and strength of the walkways showed off the potential of reinforced concrete.

Their zoo work taught Tecton the problems of using concrete as an external finish. It proved more susceptible to rainwater and air pollution than they expected. If water penetrated to the reinforcing rods or they were exposed as corroded concrete fell away, they began to rust, losing strength and expanding, setting up more stresses in the concrete, leading to accelerating deterioration.

Knowing that reinforced concrete was so strong had led architects to specify thin non-structural (and sometimes structural) walls to save weight and cost. They learned the hard way that these can be false economies. Concrete exposed to the weather has to be thick enough, mixed correctly and properly installed to protect the internal reinforcing rods.

## Sources

Allan, J. (1992), *Berthold Lubetkin. Architecture and the Tradition of Progress*, London: RIBA Publications.

Anon (2015), 'Penguin Pool, London Zoo: A Modernist Parable', *Pod Academy,* accessed 22.05.2020.

Jones, P. (2006), *Ove Arup. Masterbuilder of the Twentieth Century*, New Haven: Yale University Press.

Sambrook, J., 'Modernism at London Zoo: new ideas on housing animals', *Mid Century Magazine*, accessed 27.05.2020.

Shapland, A. and Van Reybrouk, D. (2008), 'Competing natural and historical heritage: the Penguin Pool at London Zoo', *International Journal of Heritage Studies*, **14** (1), 10–29.

The Peerage, Lt-Col. Hon. Godfrey Samuel, accessed 14.06.2020.

## GOLDFINGER SITS AT THE THEORETICAL
## HEART OF EUROPEAN MODERNISM.


Lubetkin left Perret's studio in 1926 and pitched up in London in 1931 where he founded Tecton. During that time Goldfinger was still in Paris, finally obtaining his diploma from the Beaux-Arts in 1932. Lubetkin started his professional career before Goldfinger had even qualified. Goldfinger's progress was always slow, the tortoise to Lubetkin's hare.

Like Lubetkin, Goldfinger left Perret's studio in 1926 and after graduation took part in a historic event, the fourth conference of the Congrès Internationaux d'Architecture Moderne (CIAM) in the summer of 1933. CIAM was a boosting organisation for modernist architecture, founded in 1928 by Le Corbusier and like-minded European architects, to proselytise functional design. The fourth conference was supposed to have been in Moscow, but extreme Stalinist reaction against the *avant garde* had set in and instead the organisers chartered a ship and held the conference on board, sailing back and forth between Marseilles and Athens. Goldfinger was elected secretary and took a leading part in its administration. This upset Le Corbusier, who wanted to be secretary himself so that he could keep control.

The conference took a major step forward. Architects should not confine themselves to individual buildings but plan whole towns and cities on functional principles. This was feasible in the Soviet Union, where the government had the power to knock down and rebuild cities as it pleased, but more difficult elsewhere. The opportunity arose in Europe a decade later as many cities were badly damaged by bombing, but in 1933 major reconfigurations of existing cities were pipedreams.

The conference title was 'The Functional City'. It concluded that the social problems of cities were best addressed by zoning different activities into different geographical spaces. Ideally, in the residential zone, people would live in tower apartment blocks, widely but regularly spaced and set in landscaped parkland, a similar solution to the cities of the future conceived earlier by Perret and Le Corbusier. Such top-down planning rather ignores how people actually want to live. Planning and building from theory without consulting the gorillas, penguins or people you are building for can lead to

Lubetkin and Goldfinger

disillusion and alienation. To their credit, Lubetkin and
Goldfinger were always alive to the needs of the residents
in the buildings they designed.

The issues discussed at the conference were complex
and there was disagreement and delay in publishing
reports. Eventually two large books were published, the
second being *La Charte d'Athènes* (1943), written by Le
Corbusier, essentially steamrollering his own ideas. The
charter went on to become a partially digested bible
for the post-war reconstruction of Europe's cities. In
hindsight the congress seemed to have come up with a
blueprint for the future. Goldfinger had a preview of this
urban vision and was pleased to be involved with the
core modernist thesis about urban living, which he could
partially realise in the decades after the Second World
War. For instance he made a useful contribution to
Abercrombie's plan for post-war London by co-writing a
popular account of it in 1945.

In his personal life, after free-wheeling for years as a
student in Paris, in 1931 Goldfinger met a striking young
English art student, Ursula Blackwell. She had gone to
Paris in 1928 to escape from her wealthy but conservative
background. When Goldfinger first met her, Ursula was
twenty-two, seven years his junior. Amédée Ozenfant, co-
founder of the Purist art movement with Le Corbusier,
was her Beaux-Arts tutor. Goldfinger knew Ozenfant
well and met him often. His path inevitably crossed
with Ursula's and when it did sparks flew. Goldfinger
and Blackwell were fascinated by Dada and Surrealism,
counting leading practitioners of both schools among

their friends and acquiring some of their work. They married in 1933, Ursula already pregnant with their first child. Two of the witnesses at the wedding were her older sisters who had been dispatched to Paris to rescue her from that sink of iniquity. Not only did they fail to bring her home; they colluded with her outrageous behaviour in marrying Goldfinger.

Ursula and Ernö intended to stay in Paris, but to build a home for themselves they needed to release some of Ursula's capital, tied up in a family trust. The trustees would not fund anything in France, so they decided to move to England for Ernö to build his career here. They made the move in 1934, retaining ties with Paris and friends, many of whom dispersed in the face of the Nazi threat, several winding up in Hampstead, where the Goldfingers built their house.

When they first arrived in Britain, the Goldfingers lived in Chelsea and then in St John's Wood before becoming early tenants in a Lubetkin development, Highpoint One, and then for a short while living in one of the modernist cottages Lubetkin designed for the keepers at Whipsnade Zoo. Lubetkin was already successful while Goldfinger had not started. That was another reason for not liking Lubetkin or his buildings. After 1937 Goldfinger was tied up building his own house, the central property in a short terrace at 1–3 Willow Road, Hampstead, built on modernist principles. A major unifying feature was a large concrete-framed window stretching across the front of all three properties. It produced a 'photobolic' effect, with horizontal white-painted screens reflecting light onto the interior ceilings, enhancing illumination in the north-facing rooms, a feature he introduced into many of his post-war projects. The house also had a purpose-built studio for Ursula, suggesting that she might have been a professional artist, but a demanding husband and three children in the atmosphere of the 1940s and '50s meant she became a housewife and mother.

## Sources

Carter, E.J., and Goldfinger, E. (1945), *The County of London Plan*, London: Penguin.

Gold, J.R. (1998), 'Creating the Charter of Athens: CIAM and the Functional City, 1933–1943', *The Town Planning Review*, **69**, 225–247.

Gold, J.R., 'The Athens Charter (CIAM 1933)', *Academia*, accessed 15.02.2021.

Oxford Reference, 'Overview CIAM', accessed 15.02.2021.

National Trust/National Sound Archive, *Passionate Rationalism. Recollections of Ernö Goldfinger*, undated CD.

Powers. A. (1996), *2 Willow Road*, Swindon: The National Trust.

Warburton, N. (2005), *Ernö Goldfinger – the Life of an Architect*, Abingdon: Routledge.

Wikipedia, 'Congrès Internationaux d'Architecture Moderne', accessed 15.02.2021.

*15. 2 Willow Road, the central house in the short terrace, 1–3 Willow Road. The frontage is a perfect square embracing the four piloti, the prominent uprights of the communal window and the three upper-floor windows.*

*16. 1–3 Willow Road Terrace, Hampstead, the unifying window and deep, white, horizontal 'photobolic' screens.*

## ENLIGHTENED CAPITALISTS BUILD
## MODERNIST WORKERS' HOUSING, PART 1:
## LUBETKIN TRIES AND FAILS.

In London in the 1930s Lubetkin was not the only supporter of Soviet planning; some young British architects were communists or fellow travellers. Communism was unpopular in Britain until 1941 when the USSR joined the allies against Germany. Relations with Russia stayed warm until the end of the war and the favourable atmosphere helped left-wing architects, including Lubetkin and Goldfinger, to conceive schemes for large-scale, centrally planned, post-war urban reconstruction.

Lubetkin thought architecture could transform society if there was co-operation between architects and the state. The later rise of 'post-modern' architecture, which saw no socially transformative purpose for architecture, drove him away from the frontline of the profession in the 1960s. He thought buildings should be the physical expression of architects' ideas and feelings, their personalities and psychologies made concrete. The Tecton collaboration was a paradox because Lubetkin was a loner, an *auteur*, so the partnership was really a benign dictatorship. Designs were developed by iteration, the work pattern somewhat analogous to Marxist thought. Where there was a clash of ideas/solutions to problems, *theses* and *antitheses*, the best answer, *synthesis*, logically arose from the argument between them.

Lubetkin wanted to express his socialist beliefs with large blocks of flats for ordinary people. There were already expensive, private-sector high-rise blocks set in landscaped grounds, but socialists wanted to build better flats on the same principles for workers. Modernists (rather innocently) argued that professionally kept parkland, communal central heating and a greater sense of community would outweigh the stubborn British preference for living in houses with their own gardens. Before the war there were few new blocks of flats to show working people what living in such a home might be like. Tecton wanted to use its first commission for flats at Highpoint One in North London to prove such schemes were viable. Unfortunately Highpoint turned out to be too expensive, though its modernist merits made it famous.

As with London Zoo the 1933 Highpoint commission for the Gestetner Office Duplicator Company was brokered by Godfrey Samuel. The son of the original founder of the duplicator business, Sigmund Gestetner, was in charge at the time and Lubetkin got on well with him. Sigmund commissioned Tecton to build a block of flats for his workers in the modernist style but specified an annual return on capital at the standard 'developer's equation' level. That tied Lubetkin's hands; rents low enough for workers to afford would not give such a return unless the flats were built cheaply to low standards. Lubetkin refused to do this; the whole point was to provide ordinary people with good housing. The result was a block that only middle-class people could afford, while the necessary attempts to cut costs led to shoddy construction and corner-cutting. Since the scheme proved too expensive for his workers, Gestetner's original purpose was traduced.

Lubetkin took a lot of trouble over the entrance area to make the right welcoming statement, as he had with the porches at the Gorilla House. The flats were well laid out with efficiently delivered services. Middle-class tenants were expected to have staff so there was communal accommodation on the ground floor for maids to service the flats. The block itself was cross-shaped, eight storeys high, with sixty-four units, built of cast-in-place concrete, set on Corbusian piloti and white-painted with dramatic balconies. In bright sunshine it looked like an ocean liner.

Design and construction benefitted hugely from Arup's contributions. As at the zoo, Lubetkin and Arup persuaded the authorities to waive the building regulations and allow concrete slabs to be used as structural elements. During construction they used a novel system of climbing shutters to receive the poured concrete, a time- and money-saving technique derived from civil engineering practice.

Highpoint One was well received. It was essentially *Vers Une Architecture* made flesh and Lubetkin invited Le Corbusier over from Paris to see it. Gratifyingly the master admired it and the building quickly became a modernist icon. But behind its ocean liner-like facades there were problems. Building in reinforced concrete was still experimental and cost-cutting had gone too far. The external walls were cast too thin for long-term survival or good insulation and movement in the building opened up cracks allowing water in. No one foresaw how rapidly reinforced concrete would age when atmospheric carbon dioxide reacted with alkaline concrete to produce acid that corroded the steel reinforcing rods. Long-term maintenance costs have been high. Arup knew the building standards at Highpoint One were shoddy and blamed Lubetkin for allowing them. To be fair to Tecton, in the light of their experience, the firm stopped specifying thin concrete as a facing material.

Arup thought Lubetkin dishonest for claiming that modernist design was always cheaper and more efficient than any alternative. At Highpoint One traditional brick facing would have been cheaper and not enough money was spent on the flat roofs to make them watertight. There was not much communal space, although sport and leisure facilities in the grounds were well used, but even these spaces could not act as 'social condensers', places where different classes and types of people could interact and influence each other, a Soviet constructivist concept.

Constructivists believed that buildings and towns should make the mixing of social classes inevitable to break down barriers and encourage the evolution of a classless society; physical architecture should generate social change. In 1936 Gestetner acquired the property next to Highpoint One, which was demolished and Lubetkin commissioned to design Highpoint Two. This was an altogether different proposition and any idea of workers' accommodation was forgotten. Highpoint Two wound up as twelve large duplex apartments, to be let at high rents, a long way from Lubetkin's fundamental objective of building for ordinary workers.

Highpoint Two was finished in 1938 and Lubetkin lived in the penthouse, with surrealist and ironic furnishings that he designed himself a contrast to the external austerity of the building. He designed his ideal accommodation at the same time Goldfinger was building his ideal at Willow Road. Lubetkin lived for only a decade in Highpoint in contrast to Goldfinger's half century in Willow Road. Highpoint One enthusiasts tend to be sniffy about Highpoint Two, claiming it was a backward step.

A number of well-known people have lived in Highpoint over the years, including, of course, Goldfinger and his family from 1935 to 1939. Designing and building his own house at Willow Road at the time, he tried to avoid the mistakes he thought Lubetkin had made at Highpoint.

## Sources

Allan, J. (1992), *Berthold Lubetkin. Architecture and the Tradition of Progress*, London: RIBA Publications.

Diehl, T. (1999), 'Theory and Principle: Berthold Lubetkin's Highpoint One and Highpoint Two', *Journal of Architectural Education*, **52**, 233–241.

Jones, P. (2006), *Ove Arup. Masterbuilder of the Twentieth Century*, New Haven: Yale University Press.

Lubetkin, B. (1933), 'Town and landscape planning in Soviet Russia', *Journal of the Town Planning Institute*, **19**, 69–75.

Ward, S.V. (2012), 'Soviet communism and the British planning movement: rational learning or Utopian imagining?', *Planning Perspectives*, **27**, 499–524.

*17. Highpoint One, Highgate. An ocean liner poking through the trees.*

*18. Highpoint Two, Highgate. There are no concrete facades; brick and tiles are the facing materials.*

## ENLIGHTENED CAPITALISTS BUILD
## MODERNIST WORKERS' HOUSING, PART 2:
## MAXWELL FRY (NEARLY) SUCCEEDS.

In terms of social transformation, Tecton and Lubetkin failed at Highpoint. The honour of building the first transformative modernist workers' housing in Britain rests with the British architect Maxwell Fry and social reformer Elizabeth Denby, at the Kensal House development in North Kensington completed soon after Highpoint One was finished in 1936. At Kensal House there may have been input from another modernist pioneer, no less than Walter Gropius, founder of the Bauhaus exiled to Britain from 1934 and living in the Lawn Road Flats in Belsize Park (another modernist development designed by the Canadian architect Wells

Coates). Gropius went into partnership with Fry for the two years he spent in Britain before he moved to America in 1936.

Fry and Denby had worked together on a small social housing project, R.E. Sassoon House, associated with Peckham Health Centre in South London. Kensal House was more ambitious, though many of their ideas for it were developed at R.E. Sassoon House.

The central concept was an 'urban village'. Denby was conscious that suburban cottage housing estates, the main schemes for rehousing people from urban slums, were not working. Suburbanisation destroyed the sense of community often found in densely packed terraces. Supported by a charitable donation from the philanthropist Moselle Sassoon, Denby and Fry set out to design a block of urban workers' flats. They reasoned that flats had the same tight communal spacing as terraced housing with the additional advantage of space for leisure, health and other facilities. Their developments would be partially self-contained villages within surrounding urban wastelands.

The R.E. Sassoon flats (named after Moselle's son who had been killed in an accident) were laid out for healthy living, cheerfully decorated, enjoyed good communal space with medical and social support next door at the Peckham Health Centre. Fry had been trained in neo-Classical architecture but rethought his principles in the late 1920s from reading Le Corbusier and other European pioneers. He was much impressed by the 'austere formalism and social idealism' of continental modernists.

In the 1930s the Gas Light and Coke Company (GLCC) owned a large gasworks in Kensal Town at the top of Ladbroke Grove, an overcrowded working-class area. Part of the site became vacant and the company decided to build low-rent housing for its employees there. The site was squeezed between the Grand Union Canal and the Great Western railway and included the circular base of a dismantled gasholder. Fry's practice proposed a scheme of two five-storey, white, modernist concrete blocks of flats, one curved to fit the site, with an integrated, semi-circular nursery school around the gasholder pit. The positioning of the buildings on site and layout of the individual flats were designed (as at R.E. Sassoon) for the health of the tenants. Denby made major contributions as she knew the community in North Kensington well.

The development consisted of fifty-four three-bedroom and fourteen two-bedroom flats. GLCC's motives were not entirely altruistic. All heating and other energy use on the estate was supplied by coke and gas; there were gas fires, coke fires, gas coppers for laundry, gas cookers, gas water heating and even gas-powered irons. GLCC wanted to show that a modern domestic life did not need electricity. It was trying to maintain the dominant position of gas. Such boosterism was common in the 1930s. For instance, Edgar Anstey's propaganda documentary *Housing Problems* (1935), about slum clearance and new council estates in Stepney, was sponsored by the British Commercial Gas Association and showed only gas appliances in the new flats.

At Kensal House the blocks were laid out north to south, the flats orientated with all bedrooms facing east for morning light and living spaces to the west for afternoon sun. The workspaces of kitchen, bathroom and a drying balcony were grouped together, separated from the leisure space of living room and relaxation balcony. Kitchens and bathrooms had a full range of up-to-date facilities and appliances. All flats were accessed by internal staircases, not along common walkways or balconies. The flats were small to keep rents down.

Denby also stipulated communal spaces and facilities: a nursery school, allotments, workshops and a clubroom for the social club. The community emphasis was enhanced by tenants having the major say in day-to-day running of the estate. The biggest success was the nursery school. When the estate opened in 1936 there were four hundred tenants, of whom 250 were children. Denby's motivation was Christian socialism, not the Marxist principles behind Lubetkin's housing developments.

Kensal House immediately attracted comment. It stood out as a giant 'white house' among grey terraces and crumbling hovels. Surveys revealed the majority of tenants preferred their new, well-equipped flats to the run-down housing around them. They also liked the private balconies, orientation for sunlight in all rooms, communal facilities and low rents. There were irritations. The architects applied middle-class attitudes to a working class they did not really understand and made kitchens small so that food preparation, cooking and clearing-up were as easy as possible. Such small kitchens allowed for larger living rooms. While residents liked the modern equipment, the kitchens were too small for them. Fry, and surprisingly Denby, conceived kitchens only as workspaces, analogous to workshops. The designers were deaf to the working-class culture of the tenants.

In most working-class homes the kitchen/eating area was the social centre of the home. Women were not operatives; there had to be space for social life in the kitchen with room for a communal table. The living room, usually designated a parlour in working-class homes, was kept for formal occasions and not used that much. This was irrational and wasteful and outside middle-class experience where families would spend their social time together in their living rooms. Ideally middle-class homes had two separate rooms for living and dining but already open-plan living/eating spaces were being imposed by space limitations. For the working class this space would better have been a larger kitchen/eating space.

So the best of intentions were (and are still) not always good enough. Logic and middle-class social assumptions were not the best guides to designing working-class homes. Fry and Denby's flats failed to achieve all that was intended. Nevertheless, trying to give ordinary people good housing and high environment standards was better than assembling cheap units just to give them roofs over their heads.

## Sources

Allan, J. (1992), *Berthold Lubetkin. Architecture and the Tradition of Progress*, London: RIBA Publications.

Anstey, E. Director (1935), *Housing Problems*, fifteen-minute documentary film, accessed at vimeo.com/4950031, 18.01.2021.

Darling, E. (2014), 'Building of the Month – Sassoon House, London', *The Twentieth Century Society*, accessed 08.02.2021.

Llewellyn, M. (2004), '"Urban village" or "white house": envisioned spaces, experienced places, and everyday life at Kensal House, London in the 1930s', *Environment and Planning D: Society and Space*, **22**, 229–249.

Priest, I. (2018), 'RIBA Royal Gold Medal Winner 1963, Kensal House 1936', *RIBA Journal*, accessed 19.12.2020.

Sainsbury, F., Director (1938), *Kensal House*, eleven-minute b/w documentary, The Gas, Light and Coke Company, accessed on BFI Player 21.09.2022.

Wikipedia, 'Maxwell Fry', accessed 07.02.2021.

*19. R.E. Sassoon House, Peckham.*

*20. Kensal House, Ladbroke Grove, North Kensington.*

## THE PEOPLE'S REPUBLIC OF FINSBURY 1: HEALTH CENTRES AND A VISION OF PUBLIC HOUSING.

The Finsbury Health Centre, one of Tecton's legendary achievements, still stands on Pine Street at one end of Exmouth Market in South Islington. When it opened in 1938 it was a beacon among the surrounding grimy terraces. Today it houses two doctors' surgeries and operates as a blood-taking centre. It is drab and rundown, though there is an attractive little park at the back.

In the 1930s the Labour Party began to win control of impoverished London boroughs and Finsbury came under its hegemony in 1934, aided by a handful of communists. The council leader, Harold Riley, had a vision for the borough as a paradise for working people.

He set out a grand 'Finsbury Plan' and fought hard to make it a reality. His chief ally was the Chairman of the Finsbury Public Health Committee, the Indian GP Dr Chuni Katial.

In 1932, Katial attended a British Medical Association conference where he heard Lubetkin present a Tecton design for a TB clinic, a scheme requested by the Medical Officer of Health for East Ham. The Tecton partners threw themselves into research and devised radical designs for the clinic, investigating the causes and treatment of tuberculosis and liaising extensively with public health officials. Their design provided maximum interior sunlight with controlled airflow while the movement of staff and patients was carefully zoned to minimise contact between the healthy and the sick. All the partners helped with experiments including playing with cardboard and wooden models, and carefully positioning lamps and photographic paper to work out how sunlight would penetrate the building. To explain their plans they prepared colour-coded flow charts of how people would move through the building.

The effort came to nothing; Tecton did not secure a commission, but the presentation made a deep impression on Katial. Elected to Finsbury Council in 1934, by 1936 he and Riley had drawn up their grand plan for the borough. Katial approached Tecton to design the health centre. Lubetkin got on well with both Katial and Riley, as usual because of shared politics, and Tecton generated the usual range of possible schemes. The one chosen and commissioned became an icon, but Finsbury was not alone, or even a leader, in developing such a health centre.

There were several centres in London, all designed to combine primary medical care (general practice) with public health (preventive medicine). They copied German, Swedish and especially Soviet Russian models, the latter being 'polyclinics'. Architecturally only the Peckham and Finsbury Centres were self-consciously modernist. The Finsbury Centre was originally intended as the centrepiece of the Finsbury Plan, which included new public baths, libraries and nurseries with much surrounding housing demolished and rebuilt. Before the war only the health centre was completed. After the war, the advent of the National Health Service made the London health centres redundant.

When it opened in 1938 Finsbury incorporated a wide range of facilities. It was bigger than a doctor's surgery but smaller than a hospital, planned as an attractive club to invite people in. The foyer was informally arranged with no reception desk. It was to be an education centre, a version of a Soviet 'social condenser', where all classes of people met on an equal footing. The reception area was lit through a wall of glass bricks, which Lubetkin described 'as beautiful as the hair of a beautiful young girl in the summer sunshine'. Furnishing and lighting were high quality. All the clinics were on the ground floor for easy patient access. The design built in flexibility to future-proof the building, especially the delivery of services (electricity, water and so on). Significant amounts of heating ducts and plumbing were located outside the building to keep the interior flexible.

The biggest proposed housing schemes in the 'Finsbury Plan' were at Busaco Street (later Priory Green in Pentonville) and Sadler Street (later Spa Green near Sadlers Wells). Lubetkin and Tecton based their designs on a scheme they had submitted to the Cement Marketing Company (CMC) in a competition for efficient, low-cost workers' housing to be built of reinforced concrete. They won the competition but the project was never built. By late 1938 the grand Finsbury Plan was stalled and Tecton re-focused its energies on research and design for air raid shelters. Lubetkin's council housing for Finsbury had to wait until after the war.

In the mid-1930s there was a significant change to Lubetkin's private life. Nineteen-year-old Margaret Church was instantly smitten with the thirty-six-year-old Lubetkin when she arrived for a Tecton internship. Like Ursula Blackwell, Margaret Church came from a wealthy industrial background. She was uncomfortable in her upper middle-class household. She was conscious of the poverty-stricken lives of the servants while her mother thought working people an inferior race. Margaret idolised her deceased father as a military hero and, perhaps like Ursula (who also lost her father when she was a girl) with Goldfinger, discovered a father figure in Lubetkin. Their Bohemian cohabitation in 1934/35 shocked her family. Despite her internship and later professional work Margaret never completed her architectural education. She and Lubetkin married in 1939.

Goldfinger had been active in CIAM and Lubetkin would have been a natural member of the group but did not have time for it. There were several attempts to develop a similar British group, but they all failed until the Modern Architectural Research Society (MARS) was founded in 1933 and Lubetkin joined up. He remained optimistic that the British would accept a degree of state planning, which he believed was the only way to realise a programme of general home building for the common good. The MARS Group's biggest success was an exhibition at the New Burlington Galleries in 1938 about solving the housing problems of Bethnal Green through planned redevelopment. Lubetkin was a member of MARS until 1938 and from 1934 also a founder member of the Architects and Technicians Organisation (ATO). This was a trade union rather than a pressure group. Lubetkin resisted any attempt to affiliate ATO with the Communist Party. He never lost his Marxist principles but intensely disliked the bureaucratic infighting that characterised far-left organisations. ATO was effective because it saw that solving housing and social problems needed collaboration with workers' organisations.

ATO organised a big exhibition in 1936 on working-class housing, highlighting government failure to address the need for better homes. It argued that providing such housing should be a sort of national service, dominated by a common social purpose, not individual need met by private response. Architects should be social activists, although this was at odds with their professional ethos as independent design consultants. Lubetkin believed that only public authorities had the power to ensure good standards for working-class housing, hence his keenness to collaborate with Finsbury on council housing. He could see that one logical outcome was for architects to become salaried employees of local authorities, something he was not prepared to do himself, despite his left-wing politics. After the war there was an explosion of local authority architects' departments and many younger progressive architects became council employees.

## Sources

Allan, J. (1992), *Berthold Lubetkin. Architecture and the Tradition of Progress*, London: RIBA Publications.

Gruffudd, P. ( 2001), '"Science and the stuff of life": modernist health centres in 1930s London', *Journal of Historical Geography*, **27**, 395–416.

Jones, E. (2012), 'Nothing too good for the people. Local Labour and London's interwar Health Centre Movement', *Social History of Medicine*, **25**, 84–102.

Kehoe, L. (1995), *In this Dark House, A Memoir*, London: Viking.

*Municipal Dreams* (2013), 'Finsbury Health Centre: "Nothing is too good for ordinary people"', accessed 10.02.2021.

Open University, 'Making Britain, Chuni Lal Katial', accessed 10.02.2021.

Save Finsbury Health Centre, 'History', accessed 10.02.2021.

Wikipedia, 'MARS Group', accessed 16.02.2021.

*21. Finsbury Health Centre.*

# 6

<hr>

INTERLUDE: WORLD WAR TWO. LUBETKIN
TAKES UP FARMING WHILE GOLDFINGER
ELABORATES ON ARCHITECTURAL
THEORY.


In 1938 the focus of most local authorities changed from health and housing to civil defence as war with Germany loomed. In Finsbury Alderman Riley, as Chair of the Air Raid Protection (ARP) Committee, commissioned Tecton, Arup and the Borough Engineer to design deep air-raid shelters. These proved too expensive and ran counter to Conservative government thinking, which favoured small, dispersed shelters. Deep shelters were also unpopular with the government because they were supported by left-wing councils and Marxist public intellectuals like J.B.S. Haldane and Desmond Bernal.

Churchill opposed them as he thought they would sap morale when people realised the danger of bombing.

Lubetkin pulled out of Finsbury's ARP work in 1939 when it became clear that no deep shelters would actually be built there. By that time the war had forced Tecton to stop work on the 'Finsbury Plan'. One reason Lubetkin married Margaret Church was to acquire British nationality. As a British citizen he was not forced into idleness as an enemy alien, which was Goldfinger's fate as a Polish citizen. Lubetkin took a positive role in the British war effort, though its form surprised everybody. He took up farming in the Cotswolds near Wooton-under-Edge, working in collaboration with the War Agricultural Executive Committee. Lubetkin enjoyed farming and as a communist favoured the state direction which played an increasing role in wartime. He turned one hundred acres of neglected pasture into productive arable land and quartered some exotic animals evacuated from London Zoo. He became a competent and knowledgeable farmer.

Before the war, as a Polish/Hungarian alien, Goldfinger could not be a registered architect, though he did obtain a few commissions. His only significant work was in shop design, notably the Weiss lingerie shop in Golders Green and the Abbots' children's toyshop in Wimpole Street. His immediate pre-war focus was on building 1–3 Willow Road. He originally proposed a four-storey block of flats and studios (1936), with one flat for himself and his family. That plan was turned down. As an alternative he designed a short terrace of three houses (1937), faced with London brick rather than concrete, unified by a large, apparently single window sequence on the first floor, surrounded with white-painted concrete. That plan was approved.

During the war Ernö and Ursula were active in pro-Russian activities once the Soviet Union become an ally, most famously in the 'Aid to Russia' exhibition of modern art held at Willow Road in June 1942. It raised £250 from nearly two thousand visitors for aid to Russian civilians. Goldfinger was also responsible for the pro-Soviet exhibition 'Twenty-five years of Soviet Progress' in the same year.

Otherwise he wrote technical articles on architecture, bomb damage and city planning, organised educational exhibitions and displays, and set out his theoretical credo in a series of articles for *The Architectural Review*. This wartime work pushed Goldfinger's name to the front of the modernist movement's sub-division in Britain. He made the standard modernist arguments that architecture should improve the lives of ordinary people, but the logic of efficient design should not lead to neglect of feeling. He shared a distaste for 'pure' functionalism with Lubetkin. Homes could not just be 'machines for living in'; they should induce positive emotional responses both in their own right and as part of surrounding townscapes.

Goldfinger thought occupants' emotions would best be aroused by the form of the three-dimensional space around them. While shape and size were critical, just as important were decor, furnishings and views through the windows. This was the *spatial* effect of being in the building, which was not the same as the *plastic* effect of looking at it from outside, or the *pictorial* effect of a drawing or photograph of the building. The architectural art of 'organising space' ought to produce a sense of pleasure in its occupants. Goldfinger never articulated what parameters of three-dimensional space best generated such favourable responses.

He addressed lay audiences through pamphlets and exhibitions, and took an interest in children and their education. He thought that if children were introduced to modernist design in dolls' houses they would appreciate it when they grew up, but when he made such a house for his daughter, Liz, apparently she burst into tears. He gave her a flat-roofed, smooth-walled structure while she was expecting a traditional gabled design, a house of childish imagination.

Goldfinger published pamphlets with Ove Arup on schemes for improved low-cost housing and responded positively to Forshaw and Abercrombie's *County to London Plan* of 1943 and the more elaborate document prepared by a team under Abercrombie, the *Greater London Plan*, in 1944. Development plans were drawn up for other cities as well. They all made parallel points to Le Corbusier's CIAM Athens Charter, with which Goldfinger was, of course, intimately acquainted.

The *Greater London Plan* was based on a four-ring concept. In the Inner Urban Ring there would be extensive reconstruction of bombed buildings along their original lines. New construction would be focused in the next Suburban Ring, with mixed housing and light industry, outside which was a Green Belt Ring of parkland and recreational space. Finally there was the 'Outer Country Ring', agricultural land with new-built satellite towns to rehouse the urban population that could no longer be accommodated in the reorganised city centre. This new London would only work with radical new road and rail networks. Road congestion from the uncoordinated growth of individual London boroughs had been strangling the city since the nineteenth century.

In the two inner rings, the planners aimed to reinstate older patterns of villages, which had been lost as they were incorporated into a sprawl of unplanned expansion with housing, railways, schools, factories and workshops all scrambled together. The villages were to be re-established as neighbourhoods, bounded by arterial roads taking through traffic away from the narrower streets. Planned reconstruction would provide more open space, better quality housing in the form of both terraces and tenement blocks, with industrial units all gathered in their own zone together with properly planned retail/administrative centres.

The plans were too technical to interest the lay public. Goldfinger worked with E.J. Carter to produce a popular reformulation of the *Greater London Plan* in 1945 as a Penguin paperback, *The County of London Plan*, a clear exposition and focused argument for what should be done. Goldfinger and Carter envisaged housing reconstruction as high-rise blocks of flats, ten or twelve storeys high, set in landscaped parkland, closely mirroring Le Corbusier's CIAM vision. Goldfinger was aware that flats were not popular with the British public but argued that this was because they had been poorly designed and badly built. People would not feel the same if offered well-built flats set in good landscapes. Unfortunately that assumption proved too optimistic.

## Sources

Allan, J. (1992), *Berthold Lubetkin. Architecture and the Tradition of Progress*, London: RIBA Publications.

Carter, E.J, and Goldfinger, E. (1945), *The County of London Plan*, London: Penguin.

Jones, P. (2006), *Ove Arup. Masterbuilder of the Twentieth Century*, New Haven: Yale University Press.

Keene. R. (1945), 'The Proud City, A Plan for London', documentary film made by Greenpark Productions, accessed from the Internet Archive website, https://archive.org/details/ProudCity, 21.02.2021.

Kehoe, L. (1995), *In This Dark House, A Memoir*, London: Viking.

McKellar, E. (2020), 'Designing the Child's World: Ernö Goldfinger and the Role of the Architect, 1933–1946', *Journal of Design History*, **33**, 50–65.

Powers, A. (1996), *2 Willow Road*, Swindon: The National Trust.

Project Gutenberg/World Heritage Encyclopaedia, 'Berthold Lubetkin', accessed 20.03.2021.

Warburton, N. (2005), *Ernö Goldfinger – the Life of an Architect*, Abingdon: Routledge.

Wikipedia, 'Greater London Plan', accessed 20.02.2021.

# 7

THE PEOPLE'S REPUBLIC OF FINSBURY
2: LUBETKIN SUCCEEDS BUT POST-
WAR URBAN COUNCIL HOUSING IS
UNDERMINED FROM THE START.

In 1941 Lubetkin was settling into his second career as a farmer when Alderman Riley asked him to design a monument to Lenin, which Finsbury Council intended to put up outside the house where Lenin and his wife had stayed in 1902 and 1903. They visited London again in 1905, staying in a nearby street. The Finsbury communist party had lobbied for such a plaque or tablet since 1939 but these were always refused by the London County Council (LCC).

Things were more promising once the Soviet Union joined the Allies. The LCC agreed to a tablet and Finsbury sponsored a monument. The Soviet ambassador unveiled the tablet, while Lubetkin's monument was revealed at a ceremony on Lenin's birthday. It was a cast of Lenin's head inside an angled, concrete and granite frame, set on a massive plinth, with a coloured glass panel over the head to bathe it in red light. On the plinth was a broken chain.

It was a startling monument in doubtful taste, much like Lubetkin's student project, which had him thrown out of architecture school. Lenin's head was soon defaced by fascist protesters, replaced with a duplicate and given a police guard. The bust and tablet were finally removed to storage in 1951. Lubetkin re-used the monument plinth and frame in the foundations of his flats at Bevin Court. The Cold War made Soviet communism unpopular and what was to have been Lenin Court was renamed Bevin Court in honour of a leading Labour politician.

Riley recalled Lubetkin to Finsbury in 1943 to develop Tecton's pre-war housing schemes. After the war, Riley was forced out of office for breaking money-raising rules and his grand 'Finsbury Plan' abandoned. The borough was forced into piecemeal development, starting with the Spa Green (Sadler Street) and Priory Green (Bulasco Road) Estates. Lubetkin had wanted the estates to have social infrastructure: shops, nurseries, laundries, meeting rooms and so on, which, like Fry and Denby, he considered necessary for neighbourhood development. These were cut out of the schemes to save money. Such economy severely dented Lubetkin's vision of urban public housing that was so good people would prefer to stay in the city rather than move to suburbs or out to distant towns.

Lubetkin made the facades of the Spa Green blocks as interesting as he could. A key element in his freedom to design was Arup's structural engineering. During the war Arup had proposed bomb-proof hostels for the homeless, constructed as concrete slabs and panels arranged as box frames, the square interior spaces forming rooms. Arup and Lubetkin extended the box frame concept to blocks of flats, with the structural boxes enclosing whole flats rather than individual rooms. There were three big advantages of this arrangement: no internal space was wasted on beams or columns, internal room divisions could be put anywhere, and as the external walls were not load bearing, Lubetkin could use any materials or methods he liked for the facades.

Many tenement blocks, whether modernist or traditional, were strictly functional, packing in as many flats as possible, producing massive, unsightly buildings. Windows and balconies in repetitive patterns are monotonous; there should be features to break them up. Lubetkin's solution was a checkerboard motif derived from carpet design. He had studied textiles and remembered the Caucasian carpets he had known in his youth. The checkerboard principle governed the alternating tile panel and balcony arrangements on the living-room facades at Spa Green while on the plainer, bedroom sides there were regular patterns of windows and groups of ventilation holes for the stairwells, producing a checkerboard effect over the whole facade.

Purists argued that Lubetkin was re-introducing the surface decoration that modernists rejected. Architects of later high-rise housing in Britain tended to prefer the functional elevations of Mies van der Rohe or the monumental vernacular of Le Corbusier's post-war, raw concrete-faced blocks. The latter do not work so well in Britain as grey concrete surfaces darken with rain stains and rust streaks. Strictly functional design rather ignores people's feelings. Too much modernist design was emotionally cold. Complete absence of decoration turned many people away from it while it was not all that successful in encouraging the social interaction that left-wing architects hoped would make their buildings agents of social change.

How did the Spa Green and Priory Green Estates finally work out? Spa Green was essentially a working-class version of Highpoint. The parabola penthouse on Highpoint Two, where Lubetkin lived, was re-imagined as aerofoil drying spaces atop the Spa Green blocks, while pram and bike sheds replaced the servants' ground-floor rooms of Highpoint One. The bedroom sides faced inwards, away from noisy roads. The sinuous block of Sadler House had less regular arrangements, with awkwardly placed living and bedrooms between and across flats. Here quality of internal space was sacrificed for external variety.

The flats were appointed well above usual council standards, though lagging behind the luxury at Highpoint. Spa Green made Tecton's reputation for social housing, providing a role model for future urban public housing and a prototype for three further developments from Tecton, all commissioned in 1946: Priory Green and Bevin Court in Finsbury, and the Hallfield Estate in Paddington. Tecton itself collapsed in 1948 and most of the building was overseen by a new partnership formed in 1950: Skinner, Bailey and Lubetkin.

Rapid post-war economic recovery was followed by slump in 1947 partly overcome in 1948. The building of Priory Green fell into this gap. Aneurin Bevan had planned to build fast and well, but austerity meant that after 1948 quality suffered to allow speed to be retained. At Priory Green all the planned social facilities, apart from a laundry, were abandoned and build quality reduced with simplified facades and loss of visual harmony. Access to most flats was by external galleries, not internal staircases, so the majority of flats did not have the private balconies Lubetkin originally intended. There was a considerable amount of open space, but landscaping was restricted to grass and trees. Poor build quality made this estate physically and socially hard to maintain. The estate, like many that followed, ran down quite fast.

Holford Square, one of several well-designed nineteenth-century squares in Finsbury, was severely bomb-damaged. The terraces roundabout were good quality buildings and the survivors were refurbished, as encouraged in the *Greater London Plan*, but Holford Square itself had to be completely demolished. Lubetkin designed a high-rise estate to replace it. As with Spa and Priory Greens, the original Bevin Court scheme was stripped back by lack of finance and no communal facilities were built. The first idea had been for slab blocks on three sides of the square, but this was replaced by a single Y-shaped, spoked block, an idea borrowed from Le Corbusier. All flats were accessed by open galleries; there were no private balconies, though the spokes were so positioned that no flats faced north. The estate has a reputation for light and air. Precast concrete cladding panels were used instead of tiles on the facades in another cost-saving exercise, an economy widely adopted in later blocks, both in council and private developments.

Lubetkin allowed himself complete freedom only in the central staircase of Bevin Court, a grand Piranesi concept in a large space with a huge mural acting as a social condenser to encourage interaction among residents. The whole stairwell is open plan with dramatic triangular landings and access staircases to the external galleries of the different storeys at different angles. The original colour scheme of bold red and white has recently been restored. Climbing the stairs can feel like an adventure and residents often use the stairs rather than the lifts. This central staircase, serving all three spokes of the building, is a major architectural feature exclusively for the enjoyment of the people who live there.

Imaginative council estate development, especially in the face of financial constraint, needed imaginative thinking. As local authorities built more estates they relied increasingly on in-house architects who tended to play safe and generate too many mediocre designs. Where was a practice like Tecton when it was needed? It had gone, dissolved in 1948. Professional and personal differences caused some of the problems, but there were also external forces at work. The pre-war atmosphere of novelty and excitement around council housing had gone.

Tecton's pre-war commissions had relied on close relations with discerning local authorities. After the war choice and responsibility were reined in by collective control and administration. Local authorities refused to fund development work and the Royal Institute of British Architects (RIBA) made things worse by setting lower fees for public-sector housing work. Paradoxically, central planning, advocated so strongly by Marxists and socialists, created a working environment which tended to crush the creativity needed to achieve a better world for ordinary people. Lubetkin had, of course, seen it all before in the Soviet Union.

Tecton had lost partners in a steady stream from its inception. A genuinely collaborative practice needed a leader who devolved tasks to partners with particular skills. Lubetkin was not that kind of leader. The Tecton partners surviving after the war, Drake, Skinner, Lasdun and Lubetkin, had uneasy relationships over low fees and how they were split between them. Lubetkin reduced his role with Tecton when he was hired to work on the new town at Peterlee in the summer of 1947. The young and talented Denys Lasdun, cleaving to exposed concrete and severe functionalism, was increasingly at odds with Lubetkin's design approach.

Bitterness and litigation marked the post-Tecton phase. While at the forefront of architectural design for nearly seventeen years, the practice left little obvious legacy. Whereas Le Corbusier used persuasive sketches to promulgate his design thinking, Lubetkin used verbal descriptions because he was no draughtsman. The poetry of his design and its theoretical base were difficult to express in spoken or written word.

With Tecton dispersed, a new entity had to supervise the Finsbury and Paddington estates. Spa Green was finished in 1950, but Priory Green and Bevin Court were not completed until the mid-1950s. The practice that took the projects over was Skinner, Bailey and Lubetkin. Francis Skinner (1908–98) was an original Tecton partner, sharing many of Lubetkin's strong left-wing attitudes. The Scottish architect, Douglas Carr Bailey (1915–77) was Lubetkin's chief assistant on the Peterlee New Town project which he took up in 1947. They got on well enough to enter into partnership. Lubetkin was active in this practice but not involved in day-to-day management, which fell to Skinner, who appropriately took first-name position.

Ironically Tecton and Lubetkin's legacy was perhaps best carried forward in structural engineering by Ove Arup. Arup accepted that the close relationship between form and function was a core modernist attribute but thought it ill defined. Reinforced concrete was first used in the same way as older materials with columns, piers, architraves, beams, trusses, rafters and so on, whereas it should have been seen as plastic and monolithic. For instance, huge spaces could be enclosed by curved continuous concrete of great weight saving thinness, but designing such fluid shapes demanded advanced maths, well beyond normal civil engineering or architectural expertise.

For a decade after the war Arup's consultancy struggled to survive. His strength was his personality; he could almost seduce clients into hiring his firm. He took his organisational ideas from Lubetkin and proved better able to work with and focus a team than his mentor. Through the war and afterwards he kept in touch with Lubetkin despite his move to Gloucestershire, their coolness at Spa Green, and his anger at how fast Highpoint One was falling apart.

## Sources

Allan, J. (1992), *Berthold Lubetkin. Architecture and the Tradition of Progress*, London: RIBA Publications.

Allan, J. (1998), 'Francis Skinner, Obituary', *The Independent*, 17 January, accessed 23.02.2021.

British History Online, 'London, Percy Circus Area', accessed 10.02.2021.

Dictionary of Scottish Architects, 'Douglas Carr Bailey 1915–1977', accessed 21.02.2021.

Hatherley, O. (2017), 'An Eldorado for the Working Class? The import of constructivism and the Lubetkin legacy', *Convention 2017 "Modernization and Multiple Modernities"*, KnE Social Sciences, 2018, 216–230 (DOI 10.18502/kss.v3i7.2476).

Jones, P. (2006), *Ove Arup. Masterbuilder of the Twentieth Century*, New Haven: Yale University Press.

*Municipal Dreams* (2013), 'The Spa Green Estate, Finsbury: "an outstanding advance in municipal housing… one of the showpieces of London"', accessed 15.01.2021.

Smith, A. (2015), 'Traditional square to modern classic. An area of pipes and pasture was turned into a formal square before becoming home to the striking Bevin Court', *Journal of the Islington Archaeology and History Society*, **5**, 10/11.

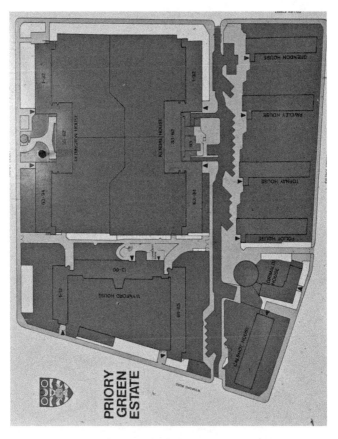

*22. Site map of the Priory Green Estate, Finsbury. The estate is large with extensive open space.*

*23. Priory Green Estate, Finsbury. Facade decoration is simple and only a few blocks have private balconies.*

*24. Priory Green Estate, Finsbury. Blocks with communal balcony galleries to the flats.*

*25. Main entrance to Bevin House, Finsbury. Behind the door a magnificent staircase gives access to the external galleries of its three wings.*

*26. Bevin House, Finsbury. Two of the angled spokes with balcony galleries in the Y-shaped building meeting over the main entrance. This front facade has decorative panelling and brickwork.*

27. *Bevin House, Finsbury. Another pair of spokes of the Y shape with flats accessed via communal galleries, not at the front so more austere.*

# 8

---

After Labour won the 1945 election, the government's major housing objective was urban reconstruction, but it proved quicker and cheaper to build new homes on greenfield sites away from town and city centres. The most extreme solutions were satellite New Towns, built beyond the green belts around London and other major cities. They were planned to be independent, attracting new industry and commerce to give local employment to new communities.

The main focus was London with a ring of towns at Stevenage, Harlow, Hemel Hempstead, Crawley, Basildon, Bracknell and Hatfield. Outside the south-east, new towns included Corby in Northamptonshire,

Peterlee and Newton Aycliffe in County Durham, Cwmbran in Wales and in Scotland, East Kilbride (for Glasgow overspill), and Glenrothes as a new town in Fife.

Blocks of flats were put up in many of these towns to create an urban feel, usually low- or medium-rise tenements, though Frederick Gibberd designing the first of these towns, Harlow New Town, experimented with the first British residential point tower. This was The Lawn, ten storeys high and oddly located in its suburban setting. New residents in Harlow and elsewhere tended to be middle-class professionals serving the new industries attracted to these towns, rather than poorer, unskilled people from the inner cities.

The town centre in Harlow, completed in the late 1950s, was underwhelming. Private-sector developers built a series of undistinguished retail and commercial blocks. Gibberd was appalled but could do nothing about it. The situation was worse in other towns, where the centres might be separated from surrounding residential areas by blank walls or encircling ring roads. Such towns could degenerate into collections of housing estates with no proper civic centre at all.

Over time New Town housing densities went up, design and build quality went down, while second-generation towns, like Milton Keynes, drew skilled people away from the original group. Harlow's industrial zone wound up in the wrong place because national transport planners moved the route of a new trunk road away from the town-planned industrial area. Gibberd bitterly remarked that it was like building a seaside town and then moving the sea. Critics of New Towns decried their low housing density, lack of urban spaces and diffuse layouts. That puzzled Gibberd, who claimed that British people liked living in suburbs and did not necessarily want the dynamism of a large town or city.

At least one New Town was intended to buck the suburban trend: Peterlee in County Durham. That difference tempted Lubetkin to have a go at town planning when the design phases of Tecton's Finsbury estates were done. In 1947 the Rural District Council at Easington in County Durham asked for a New Town to be the centre of its rural area dominated by coal mining. The coal companies had built poor quality terraced cottages round the pit heads for their workers, forming squalid villages with no worthwhile facilities and too isolated to support good public transport. Easington Council's chief engineer and surveyor, C.W. Clarke, wrote a utopian report, 'Farewell Squalor', on ways to improve the district and the lives of its inhabitants. This formed the basis of Easington's application to build a New Town.

Houses near the mines were subject to subsidence in a desolate landscape. There was no town centre so Clarke proposed to build one, to be called Peterlee, after a legendary general secretary of the Durham Miners' Association, Peter Lee. The application was successful; a Development Corporation was set up to build a town to attract new industries into the area when the coal ran out.

The first chairperson of the corporation, in 1948, was Dr Monica Felton, a Labour party activist, local councillor in London, and advisor and broadcaster on housing and public health. She had met the solicitor Lewis Silkin in the 1930s when they were both involved in LCC politics. They became firm colleagues and possibly more, despite clear differences in their political positions. Silkin was a moderate while Felton was a hard left-winger. When Silkin became the Minister of Town and Country Planning in the Labour administration in 1945, he moved Felton to better and better positions.

She was a social reformer in the Elizabeth Denby mould, focusing on social welfare in favour of women, children and family rather than men and their employment. She was intelligent but opinionated and cursed with a voice and manner that irritated her colleagues. She was not popular and subject to sexist bias.

In 1947 Silkin appointed her deputy chair of the New Town Development Corporation at Stevenage. Scarcely a year later he promoted her to the chair of Peterlee Development Corporation, which she ran from March 1948 to the end of October 1949, when she moved back to Stevenage. Life had been difficult for her in the northeast as a southern woman in an area of male-dominated heavy industry. Silkin made another radical decision in 1947: he asked Lubetkin to be Peterlee's chief architect/planner and to draw up a master plan. His appointment was confirmed in the spring of 1948.

Lubetkin had met the pair before. They had invited him to be chief architect/planner at Stevenage. He saw that the concept was a garden city and turned it down, but within weeks he had accepted Peterlee. This was different. It had been requested by a mining community and Lubetkin saw it as a 'city of miners'. He responded positively to this strong socialist vision. The coal communities wanted a proper city, away from the pit head villages and slag heaps. The industry was being radically restructured with nationalisation. Here was a real chance to do something different, looking towards a better industrial future.

Monica Felton had always consulted local people. At Stevenage she persuaded the corporation to seek advice from Professor Marshall of the London School of Economics about creating 'a balanced community' and approved the appointment of the social scientist Charles Madge, as on-site Social Development Officer, who also worked at Peterlee. Felton's combination of democratic consultation and hard-left political conviction appealed to Lubetkin. In her turn Felton liked his urban vision and they both wanted to retain the community life of the pit villages in the new town. In the end the corporation's vision did not suit the main stakeholders and it fell out with Easington Council, the village communities and the newly established National Coal Board.

Lubetkin imagined the corporation would have no shortage of materials and not be subject to the oppressive planning bureaucracy he had experienced in Finsbury. He was disappointed. He was eager to produce a master plan for the town, have it approved and push ahead. But the Ministry of Planning had agreed with the National Coal Board that the town design must take account of the underlying coal seams and the board's plans to exploit them. Building over active seams would produce subsidence, but leaving the coal in the ground would mean the community had no work. The whole project was put on hold for months. As a stopgap a 'One hundred houses' scheme was organised. The NCB agreed to find a suitable site for an immediate start on a pilot house-building exercise, but it had to be well away from any workable coal seams. The area they found was not where Lubetkin's master plan said houses should be.

In devising his plan Lubetkin had embarked, Tecton-style, on comprehensive research to create a town that satisfied local needs. Drawing on Felton's surveys, he asked how the move from villages to a large town would alter the social dynamics of the communities and how to diversify industry and create more paid work for women. How big should the town centre be and how would it communicate with the hinterland? Shops and patterns of bus routes to serve them were important. Lubetkin wanted the main A19 road to go through the town centre, not by-pass it. His reports were published in 1950 and there was considerable resistance to his analysis and proposed actions.

While a committee (the Webster Committee) investigated the tensions between the National Coal Board (NCB) and the Development Corporation, Lubetkin produced a series of outline schemes for the town, but there was still no master plan. He was bogged down in bureaucratic delay and his optimism for the project evaporated.

The Webster Committee supported the NCB position and stopped the Development Corporation building high-rise blocks of flats in the town centre. It would only permit two-storey, semi-detached houses. Lubetkin and the Development Corporation argued strongly against these conclusions, so the government set up a Regional Working Party where all interested parties could come to a compromise. They failed and in July 1949, the cabinet stepped in and dismissed the NCB case in favour of the Development Corporation. There were to be three hundred acres of stable land available for the proposed town centre, with the coal seams unexploited.

This decision did not resolve anything as the local miners turned against the scheme because the NCB warned that providing stable land meant abandoning seams and reducing employment. The general manager of the Development Corporation, A.V. Williams, was irritated by the complexity of legislation needed for Lubetkin's plan. He wanted to get the development going, even if it degenerated into a massive housing estate. He kept Lubetkin away from key meetings and insisted on appointing a consultant engineer to 'underwrite' the master plan, to take control of the project away from Lubetkin.

Meanwhile the one hundred houses project went ahead because the miners needed evidence that the scheme was not just another lack-lustre public housing development. As usual Lubetkin drew up a range of alternatives to potential planning objections, refined the design of the houses and their layout. He was sensitive to local social and vernacular needs. This scheme was finally built but only after Lubetkin had left the project.

Of his master plan, only road layouts and orientations remained. All his social infrastructure proposals for peripheral communities were excluded (no local shops, schools or community centres).

It all became impossible. He sent his resignation to Felton in November 1949, just after she had returned to Stevenage. His resignation was accepted along with that of his deputy, Douglas Bailey. Despite the delays Lubetkin did present the master plan in January 1950, with an elegant layout featuring three high-rise, point-tower blocks of flats, each twelve storeys high. The plan was never implemented. Peterlee as finally built bore little relation to Lubetkin's vision. It became a prairie suburb like many other new towns.

Lubetkin, verging on the paranoid, imagined the whole thing had been a smokescreen and no innovative new town had ever been intended. Was it just a diversionary tactic to keep the miners happy with 'jam tomorrow' while the mines were run down? He was not the man to build a new town. To persuade so many different people and interests of his vision was beyond him. He saw the project as the greatest setback of his career and it marked the start of a thirty-year partial disengagement from large-scale professional practice and public life.

## Sources

Allan, J. (1992), *Berthold Lubetkin. Architecture and the Tradition of Progress*, London: RIBA Publications.

Broughton, J. (2018), *Municipal Dreams. The Rise and Fall of Council Housing*, London: Verso.

Clapton, M. (2015), 'The rise and fall of Monica Felton, British town planner and peace activist, 1930s to 1950s', *Planning Perspectives*, **30**, 211–229.

Grindrod, J. (2013), *Concretopia. A Journey Around the Rebuilding of Postwar Britain*, Brecon: Old Street Publishing.

Peterlee Town Council, 'The New Towns Act', accessed 01.03.2021.

Vall, N. (2015), 'Two Swedish modernisms on English housing estates: cultural transfer and visions of urban living 1945–1969', *Contemporary European History*, **24**, 517–536.

# 9

---

THE LONG WIND DOWN. LUBETKIN IN THE
AGE OF HIGH-RISE COUNCIL HOUSING AS
HIS PAST CATCHES UP WITH HIM.

It can seem that Lubetkin's architectural career was over when he left Peterlee in 1950 to concentrate on farming. However some Finsbury projects were still unfinished in the 1950s and he went on to contribute to the design of more large-scale council estates in the East End. Seeing these projects to completion took him into the mid-1960s, his nominal retirement age. For fifteen years he was a part-time architect and part-time farmer, at the end farming full time for three years before he sold up and moved to Bristol.

This post-war career looked like a damp squib compared with his pre-war role as Le Corbusier's vicar in Britain. He only managed a backseat in the motorcade of high-rise council housing after the war. Le Corbusier, the master, moved on from the white-painted 'Casbah' phase to use raw concrete facades in his Unité's d'Habitation developments in France and elsewhere. The main cadre of British modernists went down this New Brutalist path. Lubetkin did not follow them.

Exposed structural concrete was logical but unfriendly and Lubetkin always wanted modernist housing to both welcome its residents and provide a bridge to the past. Many thought he had abandoned the correct modernist path. While he may not have fulfilled his early leadership promise he remained true to his principles, designing social housing of distinction. The decorated facades of his estates have survived better than many collections of raw concrete points that can disfigure our cities. Lubetkin had to cut costs and corners like the rest but managed to retain better quality and style than many of his contemporaries.

After leaving Peterlee in 1950 and a brief overseas break, he formed the new partnership Skinner, Bailey and Lubetkin to oversee the Finsbury estates and look for further work. Francis Skinner had been his closest colleague at Tecton and Douglas Bailey his chief assistant at Peterlee. The name order in the practice reflected the managerial load of the three partners: Lubetkin left most chores to Skinner and Bailey, allowing him time to farm. Nevertheless he exerted a major influence on design, with facades becoming more arresting.

In Finsbury the new practice saw Spa Green finished by late 1950. The first phase of Priory Green was completed in 1952, the second in 1957. Bevin Court was done and dusted by 1954 and the associated Amwell House finished in 1958. At the same time the partnership sought and won commissions for extensive work in Bethnal Green, another borough with overcrowded, crumbling inner-city terraces, abandoned workshops and major bomb damage. Like Finsbury it initiated ambitious slum clearance schemes and planned to rehouse many of its residents within its own boundaries, rather than building estates in the suburbs or participate in New Town schemes. Multiple high-rise estates were the inevitable consequence.

Alderman Benenson (later the founder of Amnesty International) steered Bethnal Green housing after the war. He was already a friend of Lubetkin's and persuaded his housing committee to visit four newly built estates to help them devise their own programme. One of these was Spa Green. Benenson also persuaded the committee to appoint a panel of advisory architects. Skinner, Bailey and Lubetkin were appointed to this panel in 1951 and drew up plans for the Arline Road site, eventually the core of the extensive Dorset Estate. This estate (1951–57) was the first in Bethnal Green with high-rise towers, two eleven-storey Y-shaped blocks, together with six four-storey low-rise blocks. There were 266 homes on the estate, the first in Bethnal Green built with reinforced concrete. As with the Y-shaped blocks at Bevin House in Finsbury, Lubetkin designed a dramatic staircase in each tower where the three prongs of each block met. The facades of the Dorset blocks are elaborately chequered patterns of window openings, balconies, coloured and grey concrete panels. The repeating patterns woven by these elements are elegant and complicated. The structural concrete, in egg-box frame like those pioneered in Finsbury, is not exposed to any extent. Later on a circular library and community hall were added, positioned over a basement boiler house.

In 1953 Skinner, Bailey and Lubetkin were commissioned to design the small Lakeview Estate, a double set of high-rise point towers with a small terrace of two-storey houses. The site had an awkward footprint sandwiched between a major road and a canal. The name describes its chief virtue, overlooking the green space of Victoria Park with a large lake in the western view. The estate opened in 1958. The Lakeside facades are chequered, faced with concrete panels visually separated by coloured zigzag lines, although this decoration is less dramatic than at the Dorset Estate.

In 1955 the partnership was commissioned to design the Cranbrook Estate, a giant project that took seven years to build, starting in 1961. It consists of stocky point towers in pairs, two fifteen-storey blocks, two thirteen-storey blocks, two eleven-storey blocks and five four-storey blocks together with some angled terraces of two- and four-storey townhouses and collections of bungalows for the elderly, all now arranged around a figure-of-eight road pattern. Originally there had been two strong diagonal pedestrian avenues running from corner to corner. The surrounding green space was landscaped as an integral part of the plan, with grass, trees, raised planted areas and a communal garden for elderly residents.

Once again the facades present a chequer pattern of windows, concrete panels and bas-relief coloured panels, producing visually stimulating surfaces. The north-east corner of the estate almost reaches Victoria Park and it was intended to put a path through to the park, but the council could not buy the intervening land. Lubetkin therefore created a *trompe-l'oeil* illusion that there was a path tapering into the distance covered with a series of diminishing arches, apparently mounted on blocks that served as seats. Elizabeth Frink's bronze statue 'The Blind Beggar and his Dog' (based on a local legend) sits on a plinth overlooking an ornamental pond in the garden. Commissioned by Bethnal Green Council in 1957, the statue originally stood on Roman Road in 1959 but was moved to the Cranbrook Estate in 1963.

In 1960 the practice produced the design for Sivill House, a point tower standing in Columbia Square, site of a pioneering social housing scheme by Baroness Burdett-Coutts in the early 1860s. Much decayed, this was demolished to allow the building of Sivill House, named after notable husband and wife councillors in Bethnal Green. It is a twenty-storey tower with nineteen residential floors providing seventy-six one- and two-bedroom flats, over a ground-floor entrance hall and launderette. The tower was completed in 1966. Sivill House is the only Skinner, Bailey and Lubetkin building to be listed (Grade II) in Bethnal Green (now Tower Hamlets). The flats are spacious but conventional for their time; the listing applies to the external features of the block.

The south elevation is the most dramatic, housing two-bedroom flats, in a complex pattern of brick and concrete cladding, the latter forming 'C' shapes round the windows, with a pattern break at every fifth floor for a row of narrow windows. This face has an almost woven texture; carpet designs still haunted Lubetkin. The north elevation is two parallel 'towers' of one-bedroomed flats, with east- and west-facing windows, between which is a circular stair tower, completely glazed at every fifth storey. Internally the stair tower rises dramatically from the entrance lobby. Once again Lubetkin used the stairwell for drama and intrigue.

All this inner London work was a contrast to Lubetkin's rural life, working one hundred acres of land around the hamlet of Upper Kilcott in the Cotswolds. Lubetkin treated his three surviving children badly, part of a pattern of erratic behaviour from the mid-1940s. Many of his family had gone to Poland after the First World War and were trapped in the ghetto during the Nazi era. Many of them perished and he slowly discovered details of their fate at the end and after the war. His cruelty seems to have started (or intensified) from this period. He experienced deep emotional trauma.

His daughter, Louise Kehoe, described the family's uncomfortable rural life in the 1950s and '60s. Living in rural Gloucestershire was tough. There was no electricity until 1960 and the Lubetkins refused to light fires because fireplaces were architectural monuments which had to be preserved. The only heat came from the kitchen range; laundry was hand-washed, hand-wrung and hung over the range to dry. The cold was biting and permanent. Ironically this was the sort of discomfort suffered by many poor people in unmodernised urban homes, which Lubetkin aimed to raise to good middle-class standards on his council estates.

While Margaret talked about her background, Berthold would say nothing about his. The children knew he had been raised in Russia and were told his family had been obliterated in the revolution. He even claimed Berthold Lubetkin was not his real name but one adopted to make himself seem Polish to enrol at Warsaw University. Louise left home in 1967 after the incident in Germany, but there was reconciliation in the early 1970s. Berthold was now seventy and Margaret in her mid-fifties, unwell and frail. They sold the farm and moved to a small house in Bristol, which they converted to a ground-floor flat for themselves with the upper floor to rent. Lubetkin's early works were being re-evaluated and he was sought out for interviews and invited to give lectures. But Margaret was ill, eventually diagnosed and operated on for colon cancer. Berthold would not accept that she was dying, angry with her for malingering and not trying hard enough. She died in March 1979 when Berthold was seventy-seven.

He dealt with grief by making himself busy on the

interview/lecture circuit, drinking heavily, gambling and inviting young female croupiers home with him. He still refused to tell Louise anything about his background. Only after he died in his late eighties (in 1990) did details of his early life emerge. Through contact with a cousin of her father's Louise discovered that the Lubetkins were Russian Jews. For reasons that are still not clear, Lubetkin was anxious to conceal the fact that he was Jewish. Perhaps he was trying to conceal guilt about his family's fate. If he could persuade others he was not Jewish, perhaps he could persuade himself and deny responsibility for their near-obliteration. A few relatives had stayed in Russia, including the cousin contacted by Louise. In the post-war years this cousin thought she was the only surviving family member. She hated life under communism and eventually escaped to New York.

She discovered that Berthold was alive just after Margaret had died and the pair corresponded and even met. But Berthold continued to deny he had any children, probably to prevent them and his cousin finding out about each other and revealing his Jewish origin. In terms of political philosophy, despite his dislike of the Soviet system in practice, Lubetkin remained a committed Marxist to the last.

Four years after Lubetkin died, Louise 'converted' to Judaism. He died in October 1990 and was cremated at Canford Crematorium at Westbury-on-Trym near Bristol. His family buried his ashes at an unmarked spot near the farm in Upper Kilcott.

## Sources

Allan, J. (1992), *Berthold Lubetkin. Architecture and the Tradition of Progress*, London: RIBA Publications.

British History Online, 'Bethnal Green: Building and Social Conditions after 1945. Social and Cultural Activities', website accessed 04.03.2021.

East London on Foot, Guided Walks, 'Sep 5 Lubetkin in Bethnal Green', accessed 04.03.2021.

findagrave.com, accessed 11.09.2022.

Historic England, 'Sivill House', Grade II listing, 04.06.2020, entry number 1469965, accessed 04.03.2021.

Kehoe, L. (1995), *In this Dark House, A Memoir*, London: Viking.

London Gardens Trust, Inventory Site Record, 'Cranbrook Estate, Tower Hamlets', accessed 04.03.2021.

Roman Road London, 'The History of the Cranbrook Estate, from slums to utopian post-war housing', accessed 04.03.2021.

Wikipedia, 'Cranbrook Estate', accessed 04.03.2021.

Wikipedia, 'Dorset Estate', accessed 04.03.2021.

Wikipedia, 'Lakeview Estate', accessed 04.03.2021.

Wikipedia, 'Sivill House', accessed 04.03.2021.

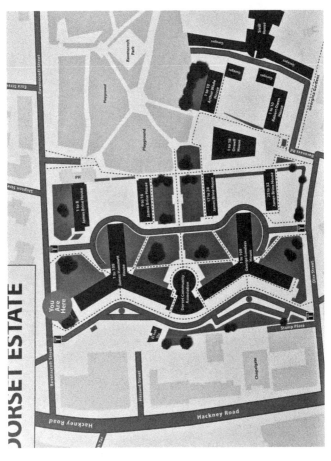

28. *Site map of the Dorset Estate showing the two dominant Y-shaped blocks.*

29. *Loveless House, Dorset Estate, Bethnal Green. Intricate facade decoration.*

*30. Cranbrook Estate, Bethnal Green. Monolithic high-rise blocks.*

*31. Cranbrook Estate, Bethnal Green. Extensive network of middle-rise blocks.*

*32. Stairwell, Mödling house, Cranbrook Estate, Bethnal Green. A relatively subdued example of Lubetkin's love of staircases.*

*33. Southern facade of Sivill House, Bethnal Green. More intricate facade decoration.*

34. *Northern aspect of Sivill House, Bethnal Green. Twin towers joined by a circular stairwell.*

# 10

GOLDFINGER EASES AHEAD, FINALLY
ACHIEVING HIGH-RISE LIFT-OFF IN THE
1960S.

Lubetkin's best professional years were from the mid-1930s to 1950. He rather fell off a cliff at Peterlee and then slid into modest decline with the Bethnal Green estates. After helping to invent high-quality, high-rise urban council housing and designing some of the best, he could not retain his lead. The hare ran out of steam.

Goldfinger had a different trajectory. He was close to the driving seat at the 1933 CIAM conference where the blueprint for much post-war city planning was developed. He wrote about the virtues of high-rise council housing in the architectural trade press during the war as well as co-authoring the most accessible version of the *Greater*

*London Plan.* He should have been well placed to take a major role in the post-war high-rise council-housing boom. But nothing happened. He could not secure anything meaningful at the Festival of Britain in 1951, though two of his ex-assistants, Ralph Tubbs and Jim Cadbury-Brown, were very active. The small Goldfinger practice stumbled through the 1950s. He could not realise the Perret and Le Corbusier-inspired vision of high-rise housing set in urban parks. Only when the sun was setting on this vision was he able to design two such estates in Poplar and North Kensington in the late 1960s. He blossomed only when Lubetkin's career was virtually over.

Goldfinger was finally naturalised as a British citizen in 1947, allowing him to participate fully in professional life, although he found he could only secure commissions through his left-wing connections. In association with Colin Penn he designed the rebuilt *Daily Worker* offices in Farringdon Road and the Communist Party Headquarters in Covent Garden. Penn was an active communist and had been chief assistant to Chermayeff on the De La Warr Pavilion at Bexhill in the 1930s.

Goldfinger also designed two London primary schools completed in 1950. He built a further school, finished in 1963. One of the first two schools, Greenside Primary School (originally Westville Road School), in Shepherd's Bush, was listed in 1993. It stands on the site of an earlier school destroyed by bombs. The LCC first proposed a temporary solution to the post-war shortage of school buildings by making use of redundant

Ministry of Works huts. Instead Goldfinger proposed cheap permanent buildings costing little more than the temporary huts, which secured him the first two commissions.

In both cases the buildings have frameworks of precast, reinforced concrete slabs and panels. On some walls the facades are glazed, the windows fitted into squares formed by the frame; others are brick infilled. Greenside has a fully glazed assembly hall, connected to the main building by a covered walkway. There is also a tall H-shaped brick tower by the entrance, for which Goldfinger commissioned a mural from Gordon Cullen with whom he had worked on educational exhibitions during the war. For a long time this mural was covered up, but it was restored and unveiled in 2014.

Goldfinger designed some small office blocks in the 1950s, notably at 45/6 Albemarle Street in London's West End, an infill where two Georgian buildings had been bombed. The building integrates well with the older architecture of the rest of the street. The front facade is clad with Portland stone over its concrete frame with extensive steel-framed windows. The pattern on the rear facade is similar but finished in bush-hammered concrete. The front elevation has two steel-framed, projecting oriel windows and the rest of the front glazing has 'photobolic' screens, first used at Willow Road before the war. The lower parts of the windows are set forward, flush with the facade, while the upper portions are set back into the office on light-diffusing white screens. Light falls on these screens and is reflected onto the interior ceilings.

The listing document describes 45/46 Albemarle Street as 'one of the most distinguished office buildings of the 1950s'.

He designed another London infill, this time residential, commissioned in 1952 and completed in 1956, a four-storey block of flats and studios at 10 Regents Park Road in Primrose Hill. Pauline and Harry Baines, with like-minded friends, formed themselves into a housing society to raise a 90% mortgage to pay for construction. As with Albemarle Street, bomb damage had destroyed two houses, this time in a stuccoed mid-nineteenth-century terrace. With economical internal arrangements, Goldfinger squeezed in ten flats and studios together with four garages. The co-operative admired Goldfinger's simple, space-saving interior designs, sparsely equipped with high-quality floor coverings and fittings.

The block has a concrete frame of three load-bearing walls, the back external facade and two internal walls on either side of the central stairwell. The front facade is a concrete beam and column construction, finished in brick and concrete panels, with balconies, the concrete frame exposed to the surface. He boldly used brick despite this infill being in a white, stuccoed terrace. The adjoining houses do not match up so Goldfinger lined up the cornicing on his building with the existing house to the right and his projecting balconies with the house to the left. He allowed the concrete framework greater surface exposure than before and it became a feature of his later, large-scale buildings. One of the original commissioners, Pauline Baines, was a designer and art director for Thames and Hudson and lived in her flat for over sixty years. She died in January 2021, aged 103.

On the domestic front Ernö's mother arrived from Paris in the mid-1950s after his father died. Frail and tiny, she lived on the top floor of 2 Willow Road for many years until she died at 101. His Jewish parents had somehow survived the war unharmed in Nazi-dominated Europe, probably in Romania. Nobody knows quite how this happened. Their survival was a contrast to the fate of Lubetkin's family.

While Goldfinger designed affordable housing in the 1950s little was actually built and planners often altered the little that was put up, destroying his design concepts. Conservative planning committees were the bane of his life. He had a famous spat in Hampstead in 1958 over plans for a block of flats in the Vale of Health. There was strong opposition from the Old Hampstead Group, but he won his case, though the development was never built because the clients lost interest.

He designed a group of big-scale office blocks when the Elephant and Castle area in South London was redeveloped in the 1950s. This was a speculative development by Arnold Lee, who had commissioned 45/6 Albemarle Street. At an early stage the Ministry of Health took over the whole complex and named it Alexander Fleming House. The site was awkward, squeezed between Newington Causeway, New Kent Road and a major railway viaduct. Four blocks surrounded a central square and were of different heights to create an interesting profile, the tallest being eighteen storeys.

Concrete frames were exposed across the blocks, bush-hammered, with brick and concrete panel infills and extensive glazing. As at Albemarle Street he created visual interest on the facades by bringing some of the bays forward: a modernist form of oriel window. He also made use of the 'photobolic' effect again, with white-painted screens across the north-facing windows with casements set back above to reflect light onto the interior ceilings. The Ministry of Health vacated the building in 1989 and it stood empty for a dozen years until converted into residential flats as Metro Central Heights from 2002.

Alexander Fleming House was praised by architects but hated by its occupants for poor temperature and humidity control, leaks, and a host of other maintenance issues. Some of this was caused by design errors, but poor build quality was also responsible. Eventually the combined faults produced 'sick building syndrome', a feature of many blocks of this era, forcing the bureaucrats out. The refurbishment work for residential use has cured most of these problems. Goldfinger also designed the nearby Odeon Cinema (now demolished), an entirely functional building that did not mimic a theatre.

Goldfinger's high-rise council housing ambitions were finally realised with the twenty-seven-storey Balfron Tower in Poplar at the northern end of the Blackwall Tunnel, completed in 1967 and occupied from 1968, part of a three-phase high-/middle-/low-rise development for the LLC in this deprived area. Most residents came from locally cleared slum terraces. A separate service tower is linked to the residential block by flexible, largely glass walkways three floors apart. The service tower has military connotations: sheer concrete walls, openings like arrow slits, severe top overhang. The facades of the residential block are not uniform; Goldfinger introduced visual interest at close quarters to mark key floor heights.

Balfron Tower was the first of three phases on the Brownfield Estate (originally Rowlett Street). Goldfinger was engaged in 1963, although now approaching normal retirement age. Phase One at Brownfield comprised Balfron Tower, old people's housing and a shop (1965–67). Phase Two was the middle-rise Carradale House (1967/68), while Phase Three was another middle-rise, Glenkerry House (1972–75), with a community centre and some low-level blocks. A nursery school completed the thin communal facilities. The basic features of Balfron Tower were based on his designs for a council-housing scheme at Abbots Langley in Hertfordshire, of which only three- and four-storey maisonettes and flats were built, not the thirteen-storey slab he envisaged at the core. This un-built block was designed with a detached staircase and service tower, while interlocking flats in the residential block opened onto single internal corridor/galleries at every third storey.

The design of separate service tower and residential block presented a unique outline and, according to the LCC's chief in-house architect at the time, was a 'landmark' building where 'a high sense of visual drama would be achieved while emerging from the Blackwall Tunnel'. The tower contained 136 one- and two-bedroomed flats, and ten maisonettes arranged over twenty-six storeys. There are six flats on each floor, apart from five maisonettes on floors one and two, and another five on floors fifteen and sixteen. These two distinct bands of glazing/balconies on one outside face of the tower break the monotony of otherwise regular facades. There are large windows; all units had balconies with timber cladding providing visual interest. The framework is carefully detailed, bush-hammered, reinforced concrete. It was occupied largely by families, so there were many children and teenagers living there. Confined to two bedrooms with small balconies, these flats were not really big enough. Public-sector budgets seldom allowed flats large enough for families.

The 'galleries' within the block and along the service walkways only worked partially as substitute 'streets' for the terraces the residents had left behind. Goldfinger envisaged that people would sit in their doorways and chat as they had in their old homes. He was more conscious than most architects of working-class culture but did not really understand it. He and other high-rise enthusiasts saw the domestic skyscraper as a 'vertical village', reflected in the choice of name for the tower 'Balfron' after a Scottish village (Poplar had attracted a large Scottish population to work on the waterfront in the nineteenth century). Since floors were filled with people moved as far as possible from the same street, reasonable social integration across households was maintained.

The service tower contained two access lifts, central heating boilers, water pumps, fire pumps and rubbish chutes. The idea of the separate tower was to insulate service noise and disruption from the flats. These were particular problems of high-rise buildings in the 1950s and '60s, where noise and vibration could be heard and felt throughout the building. The Balfron flats were well insulated with nine-inch concrete walls to the sides and twelve-inch concrete slabs under floors and above ceilings. The service tower was substantial enough to contain community facilities such as laundries, sports, club and hobby rooms, some designated for young people, features omitted from most developments. There was sharp contrast between the glazed and balconied residential block and the fortress-like service tower. The nine walkways connecting the towers at every third floor gave onto galleries with eighteen entrance doors to three floors of flats. This was intended to increase the chances of social contact. Another reason for having only nine access levels was to speed up the lifts.

Goldfinger used Balfron as the basis for his thirty-one-storey Trellick Tower on the eleven-acre Cheltenham (Edenham) Estate in North Kensington. In 1963 the terraced housing in this area was declared unfit and scheduled for redevelopment after the LCC was transformed into the Greater London Council (GLC). Goldfinger was engaged in 1967 and the estate built between 1969 and 1973, with a generous four acres of designated open space. The estate consisted of five rows of thirty-four terraced three-storey townhouses, two six-storey blocks of flats (one of thirty-six units, the other with thirty) grouped together, separated by the open space from Trellick Tower, which stood on a very narrow footprint. There are 317 dwellings in total, 217 in Trellick Tower, mainly one- and two-bedroom flats with five maisonettes and two one-bedroom flats on the twenty-third and twenty-fourth floors. The ground floor had six shops, an office, and youth and women's centres. There was also a doctor's surgery. The design and construction of Trellick closely followed Balfron, this time four storeys taller with a slimmer service tower having a large, overhanging, glazed boiler room at the top. The changes in proportion produced a better-looking building.

Rapid social deprivation turned Trellick into the 'Tower of Terror', much to Goldfinger's distress. His main proposed solution was proper security with concierges, which the GLC refused to fund. The whole estate and stairwells, chutes and corridors were open to the public and not overseen. Vandalism and violence followed; unlocked fire hydrants were simply asking to be turned on. Stairwells became slum-like haunts for drug dealers and prostitutes. Rough sleepers and muggers occupied the warmed corridors, and more articulate tenants refused to go there, leaving essentially 'problem' families behind. The park areas were not landscaped properly. The blocks were located in areas of existing social deprivation and criminal activity, and architecture alone cannot reverse these trends.

The main case against tower blocks is their anonymity, lack of surveillance and multiple escape routes. But these deficiencies can be overcome, and they have been at Balfron and Trellick Towers with concierges, CCTV, limiting access routes and the formation of tenants' associations with real influence over how the estates are run.

There was no more high-rise council housing in the 1970s and '80s. Goldfinger himself became more politically conservative but was unswerving in his enthusiasm for reinforced concrete. Until the day he died he had one of Auguste Perret's hats on a prominent shelf in his office, to remind him of his debt to that master.

He was never honoured but, supremely confident that he was an important architect, gave his entire professional archive to RIBA. He and Ursula often visited to sort out the mass of plans and models. His reputation began to revive in the late 1980s but rather too late for him. In the mid-1980s he was diagnosed with pancreatic cancer, dying after painful debilitation at Willow Road on 15 November 1987 at eighty-five years old. He was cremated and there is no memorial or gravestone.

## Sources

Braghieri, N. (2019), 'The Towers of Terror: A Critical Analysis of Ernö Goldfinger's Balfron and Trellick Towers', *Urban Planning*, **4**, 223–249.

British Listed Buildings, '45-46 Albemarle Street', listed April 1991, accessed 19.03.2021.

British Listed Buildings, 'Carradale House, Lansbury, Tower Hamlets', listed December 2000, accessed 19.03.2021.

Designing Buildings Wiki, 'Ernö Goldfinger', accessed 19.03.2021.

Greenside Primary School Online Prospectus, 'Building', accessed 19.03.2021.

Historic England, 'Balfron Tower', listed March 1996, accessed 19.03.2021.

Historic England, 'Cheltenham Estate', listed November 2012, accessed 19.03.2021.

Historic England, 'Greenside School, Westville Road W12' listed March 1993, accessed 19.03.2021.

Historic England, '10, Regents Park Road', listed December 1998, accessed 23.03.2021.

Historic England, 'Metro Central Heights', listed July 2013, accessed 19.03.2021.

Historic England, 'Trellick Tower Cheltenham Estate', listed December 1998, accessed 18.03.2021.

Hollingsworth-Hallett, A., '45 Albemarle Street W1, 15 November 1940', *West End at War*, accessed 19.03.2021.

Manchester History, 'Carradale House, Poplar', London, accessed 19.03.2021.

National Trust/National Sound Archive, *Passionate Rationalism. Recollections of Ernö Goldfinger*, undated CD.

Redhouse, R. (2021), 'Obituary, Pauline Baines', *The Guardian*, Journal Section, 9.

Roberts, D. (2015), *Balfron Tower, a Building Archive*, Ernö and Ursula Goldfinger, 1968, and Oldham, R. (2010), 'Ursula Goldfinger's Balfron Tower Diary and Notes', courtesy of the Twentieth Century Society, accessed 19.03.2021.

Twentieth Century Society (2014), Bullen, A., 'Building of the Month, Trellick Tower, London', accessed 18.03.2021.

Twentieth Century Society (2019), 'C20 Society's fear are confirmed as the Balfron Tower's new look is unveiled', accessed 19.03.2021.

Warburton, N. (2005), *Ernö Goldfinger – the Life of an Architect*, Abingdon: Routledge.

35. *Greenside Primary School, Shepherd's Bush. Buildings peeking out over the high protective wall.*

*36. Greenside Primary School, Shepherd's Bush. The brick tower by the main entrance.*

37. 45/6 Albemarle Street, Central London. Oriel windows and 'photobolic' screens were used repeatedly on the much bigger Alexander Fleming House project.

*38. 10 Regents Park Road, Primrose Hill.*

*39. Metropolitan Heights (Alexander Fleming House), Elephant and Castle.
Dramatic wing over the street.*

40. *Metropolitan Heights (Alexander Fleming House), Elephant and Castle.*
*Slabs of different heights to create an interesting profile.*

*41. One entrance to the Brownfield Estate, Tower Hamlets. Middle-rise block, low-rise terracing and Balfron Tower.*

*42. Brownfield Estate, Tower Hamlets. Geometry of Balfron and Carradale Houses.*

*43. Trellick Tower, Cheltenham Estate, North Kensington.*

# 11

HIGH-RISE FALLS IN THE REACTION
AGAINST MODERNISM.

Sir Patrick Abercrombie was kept busy in the mid-
1940s. Not only did his team prepare *The Greater
London Plan*; they also produced reports for provincial
cities, many badly bomb-damaged and with the same
long-standing housing, pollution and transport problems
as London. Abercrombie consistently suggested the
same solutions: zoning to keep industrial, residential
and commercial activities apart; massively improved
transport systems to make movement for trade;
commerce and leisure more efficient; and extensive
building of new homes, some on pre-war residential
footprints, ideally with high-rise blocks.

Sick of dark and dirty Victorian decay, architects,

planners, politicians and the public all wanted refurbished
and new buildings to be 'modern': light, simple, efficient,
uncluttered – all features promised by building with
the modernist emphasis on function. Nearly everybody
supported the wholesale clearance of slums and their
replacement with modern homes, although doubts
began to creep in once progress was made on the
greenfield towns and suburban estates in the 1950s.
Some new housing (both private and public) was badly
designed and shoddily built. Local authority architects
and planning departments proved conservative and
too much design was dictated by the private-property
developers working with local authorities.

One of the cities over which Abercrombie ran his
slide-rule was Bath, a place that had slumbered through
the first half of the twentieth century as a residential town.
It was no longer the exciting spa and resort city it had
been in the eighteenth and early nineteenth centuries.
The torpor meant that its network of fine Georgian
housing had remained largely intact until two major
bombing raids in 1942, revenge attacks for British raids
on historic German towns. These left a trail of damage
to the historic core of the town, stimulating the council
to commission Abercrombie to advise on rebuilding and
redevelopment.

Everyone realised the importance of preserving the
best Georgian buildings. In 1937, a full decade before it
was introduced nationally, Bath set up a listing system
to identify buildings of historic significance and impose
limits on how they could be altered. There were over a

thousand items on the list and quite a few were badly damaged in the 1942 raids. It was agreed that they should be rebuilt as closely as possible to their pre-war selves, but in the spirit of the new age the city plan envisaged taking out large swathes of less important buildings for reconstruction and surrounding the city with big roads and roundabouts. Even the mews houses behind the famous Royal Crescent were to be partially demolished to make way for a civic centre. In the end, not much of Abercrombie's vision was actioned apart from rebuilding war-damaged grand housing and putting up suburban cottage council estates on the city outskirts.

Bath was a pleasant place to live and attracted affluent residents. Most of the townhouses, built in an austere Palladian style, were too big and expensive for even up-market residents and were mostly divided into flats. The conversions were often poorly done, but residents put up with them (and the toxic problem of car parking) for the pleasure of living in such a beautiful place. Car ownership was rising fast and the main A4 from London to Bristol went right through the middle of the city. The traffic was intolerable by the late 1950s. The motorway network that would take much traffic away was still at the planning stage and the city lies in a bottleneck on the River Avon surrounded by steep hills, so there was no room for a by-pass.

The city fathers dusted down their Abercrombie and in 1963 commissioned the transport planner, Colin Buchanan, to prepare another report in 1965: *Bath: A Planning and Transport Study*. He advocated solving the traffic problems by running a road tunnel under the centre of the city, its over-ground approaches cutting through historically interesting inner regions. Armed with Abercrombie and Buchanan the local authority accelerated the wholesale demolition and rebuild of swathes of the inner ring area of the city for modern housing and a new retail centre. So dramatic were the changes they triggered a great deal of local opposition, countered by the planners with comments like 'if people want to live in Georgian buildings then they had better live as Georgian artisans did', a clear articulation of a modernist cliché, that a modern life needed modern infrastructure, despite the evidence of successful adaptation of old housing stock from many converted townhouses. By 1968 the tide was turning and Buchanan produced a second report: *Bath: A Study in Conservation*.

But the modernist leviathan blundered on. An early harbinger was the modernist Frederick Gibberd's City of Bath College building (1957–63) standing out like an angular boil in its bomb-damaged Georgian surroundings. Gibberd was shocked to receive insults and objections from those he considered architecturally ignorant. Vast tracts of the commercial and industrial areas by the river in the south of the town centre were demolished for the Southgate shopping centre which emerged in the late 1960s, itself in turn demolished and rebuilt in pastiche Georgian in the early twenty-first century. The old riverside industrial area to the west of Southgate remains blighted to this day, a set of bleak car parks. Where the proposed Buchanan tunnel was to plunge under Bath by Walcot Street saw the construction of an obtrusive hotel (1973) perched over a nasty multi-storey carpark, alongside pastiche classicism in the Podium Building (1974), now a supermarket.

These were isolated excesses. What finally drove oppositional conservation into life was the widespread destruction of modest artisan terracing, much of it Victorian but following the austere proportions of its grander Georgian and Regency predecessors. These buildings might well have been listed in a city without a Palladian core.

It is now quite hard to grasp how deep the modernist mindset had penetrated the popular psyche and just how virulent opposition had to be to overcome it. My generation benefitted from the long neglect of much Victorian, Edwardian and earlier housing in the post-war years and could afford to buy historically interesting terrace houses and cottages in the late 1960s and early 1970s. They usually needed major restoration, but their defects could be corrected. It was clearly not necessary to demolish proto-slums and start again. One of the first things we baby boomers did was rip out the hardboard or plywood sheeting that had been applied to panelled doors or to block up fireplaces. Such tokenism was nearly universal as earlier residents had tried to make their homes more 'modern' by smoothing off the surfaces. The fact that so many young Turks reversed this trend showed how post-war generations did not much like blanket modernism and were eager to dig into history.

The mid-century revulsion at Victoriana was well and truly over.

By 1970 quite a lot of the historic artisan terracing in Bath had been replaced by modernist 'villas' and apartment blocks, one of them a high-rise point tower above the London Road. These new homes lacked the 'character' of the housing they replaced. Over time these buildings have developed their own character and do not grate so badly with the Georgian centre. Nevertheless we can mourn the loss of much interesting housing. In some cases the new 'accommodation units' were intertwined with real Georgian treasures, notably the Ballance Street redevelopment between Lansdown and Julian Roads. This consisted of hulking multi-storey tenements let into a steep hillside, replete with dark mansard roofs, the universal feature of modernist civic development in Bath, reflecting the mansard roofs of many Palladian terraces. At least (with some effort) a real tennis court from the eighteenth century was preserved and the terraces of nearby Morford Road were kept, though they had all been emptied out in preparation for demolition and badly damaged in the few months they were abandoned, making them more expensive to renovate.

The conservationists in Bath and elsewhere fought an uphill battle against the entrenched power of commercial developers, compliant local councils and the modernist architectural establishment, but they eventually won. After the 1970s, the worst demolition in Bath stopped but the history of development over the past fifty years has been mixed.

Bath was a pivotal case in the turn against modernism and the rise of conservation movements determined to stop the destruction of the past. Here the elegance of Palladian civic housing came face to face with its re-expression in modernist aesthetics. Modernism suffered in Bath because it was mediocre. Modern buildings competently but unimaginatively assembled by the civic architecture department were up against type specimens of Palladian excellence in John Wood's squares, circuses and crescents. The modernist case was not well made; adjacent Georgian and modern buildings do not have their prominent elements lined up between old and new, something which a careful modernist like Goldfinger always considered when he designed infills.

Goldfinger and Lubetkin were seldom doctrinaire. Full-strength modernism often arrogantly ignored context. Since demolition and a clean slate are seldom possible, integration is essential, as is emotional warmth in the form of buildings, their facades and the interior layout of apartments and communal spaces. Too many modernists ignored these subtle issues and argued for the logic of their designs; reason was to trump feeling. Too few architects would compromise; too few developers and planners could be bothered to take the trouble to think about the social and community needs of council residents. Two of those who did, Goldfinger and Lubetkin, were cast aside with the rest when the reaction against modernism, and its most iconic expression, the tower block, took off.

## Sources

Bath Preservation Society, 'Brutal Bath. Explore the Post-War Architecture of Bath', Bath: Tourist Leaflet.

Fergusson, A. (2011), *The Sack of Bath*, London: Persephone Books (orig published 1973 and reprinted 1989 by Michael Russell).

Forsyth, M. (2007), *Pevsner Architectural Guides, Bath*, New Haven and London: Yale University Press.

Museum of Bath at Work (2013), 'The Best for the Most with the Least. Council Housing in Bath 1945–2013. A Social History'.

*44. North side of Queen Square, Bath. John Wood's high point of Palladian elegance.*

45. *Early modernist council housing in central Bath.*

*46. Modern apartment blocks rub shoulders with artisan terracing.*

47. The 'Hulking' Balance Street Estate abuts late Georgian Portland Place.